Teach Me
SPORTS
BASEBALL

By Barry Dreayer

General Publishing Group, Inc.
Los Angeles

Publisher: W. Quay Hays
Editor: Barry Dreayer
Managing Editor: Colby Allerton
Cover Design: Kurt Wahlner
Production Manager: Nadeen Torio
Copy Editor: Charles Neighbors

The publisher and authors wish to thank the following for
their contributions: Vicki Blumenfeld, Tom Hufford, Paul
Joffe and Kassandra Smolias.

The Teach Me Sports™ series is published by General Publishing
Group, Inc., 3100 Airport Avenue, Santa Monica, CA 90405
310-915-9000.

Library Catalog Number 94-075775
ISBN 1-881-649-34-2

10 9 8 7 6 5 4 3 2 1

Printed in the USA

INTRODUCTION

Those who have grown up with America's Pastime may not comprehend that some people have no idea what baseball is all about. Others may have acquired a basic understanding of the game while being confused by many of its finer points.

This book begins with the assumption that the reader is aware that baseball involves "players wearing uniforms who (at appropriate times) hit a ball with a bat, run, throw, and catch the ball with a glove." From this basic premise, the book presents a crash course on becoming an educated baseball fan. It is meant to be used while watching the games on TV and/or in person.

This book does not attempt to cover every one of baseball's thousands of rules and situations, and many examples have been simplified for the sake of clarity. The text shows the WHY behind the WHAT. (For example: why a team manager or coach almost always chooses to pinch hit a left-handed batter against a right-handed pitcher.)

So, come on and join the fun by learning the game!

Teach Me SPORTS
JOIN THE FUN BY LEARNING THE GAME

THE BASEBALL EDITION

THE ORIGIN OF BASEBALL

No one knows for sure who actually invented the game of baseball. Many people side with the fable that Abner Doubleday is the "father of baseball." This theory is based on the results of the Mills Commission that was appointed by Albert Spalding in 1907.

The Mills Commission's report is based primarily on the testimony of Abner Graves, an 80-year-old man who told Abraham Mills of the commission that Abner Doubleday invented baseball in Cooperstown, New York, in 1839. Evidence has since developed that contradicts Mr. Graves' testimony. At the time Doubleday was supposed to have invented the game in Cooperstown, he was actually attending West Point. Also, Doubleday never mentioned baseball in his memoirs, nor was it indicated in his obituary.

Most historians believe baseball was created by Alexander Cartwright, a bank teller, in 1845. The first game was played on June 19, 1846, in Hoboken, New Jersey. The rules dictated that the first team to score 21 won the game. Also, it was permissible to throw the ball at the opposing players to get them out. Gloves were not used, and if a ball had been caught on the first bounce, it was treated as if it was caught in the air. Like modern-day, slow-pitch softball, pitches were thrown underhand.

Over the next century and a half, baseball evolved into the modern-day version enjoyed by millions.

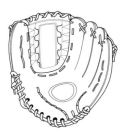

*During the seventh inning of a base-
ball game, it is a tradition for fans in
the stadium to stand up and "stretch"
before their team bats. The most
popular theory suggests that the
SEVENTH-INNING STRETCH started in
1910, when President William
Howard Taft stood up to stretch himself in the seventh inning of a game.
Thinking that the President was leaving, the fans stood up out of respect.*

BASIC RULES AND OBJECTIVES

The team with the most points (called RUNS) scored at the end of the game wins. In a game each team can "fail" 27 times.

- ◆ Each time a team fails, this failure is called an OUT.
- ◆ Outs are grouped by threes (for each team) into INNINGS. There are 9 innings in a game (3 outs X 9 innings = 27 outs).
- ◆ In the following situations, a team may have more or less than the normal 27 outs in 9 innings:
  - If the score is tied after 9 innings, EXTRA INNINGS are played until one team scores more than the other, with the home team having the last chance.
  - If the HOME TEAM is winning after its 8 innings, and the VISITING TEAM has already had 27 outs, the home team does not use its last three outs, since it has already won the game.
  - If a game must be stopped after at least 5 innings have been played (usually because of rain), it is still an OFFICIAL GAME that counts in the standings. In this case, if the home team is winning after its 4 innings, and the visiting team has already had its fifth inning, the game can be declared official.

The LINE SCORE below summarizes the scoring of a typical game: the Atlanta Braves scored a total of 5 runs, while the visiting L.A. Dodgers scored 3 runs. The "X" in the "bottom half" of the 9th inning indicates that Atlanta did not use its final 3 outs, since it had already won the game when L.A. failed to tie or take the lead in the "top" (their half) of the 9th.

TEAM	INNING		
	123	456	789
Los Angeles	030	000	000
Atlanta	000	040	01X

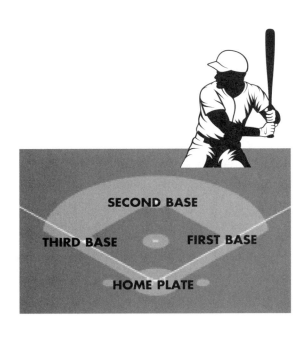

A player's main objective is to begin at HOME PLATE and advance around the four BASES without making an out. When a player safely touches the fourth base (returning to home plate) his team scores a RUN. The team with the most runs at the end of the game wins.

- ◆ To begin the "trip" through the bases, a player must initially reach first base without using up an out. Here are the ways that can be accomplished:
  - – HIT — The person with the bat (the BATTER or HITTER) hits a pitched ball (so that the opposing players on the field cannot catch it) and arrives at first base before the ball is in the possession of an opposing player touching first base.
  - – WALK — A pitched ball is thrown four times to the batter (who does not attempt to hit the ball) outside of the STRIKE ZONE (the area above home plate between the top of the batter's knees and bottom of his armpits). This type of pitch is called a BALL. Four of them to one batter is referred to as a BASE ON BALLS or WALK.
  - – HIT BY PITCH — The batter is hit by a pitched ball.
  - – CATCHER'S INTERFERENCE — As the batter swings the bat, it touches the catcher (usually his glove).
  - – DROPPED THIRD STRIKE by the catcher — Discussed in detail later.
  - – ERROR — The batter hits a pitched ball that is misplayed by an opposing player (FIELDER), enabling the batter to arrive at first base before the ball is in the possesion of an opposing player touching the base.

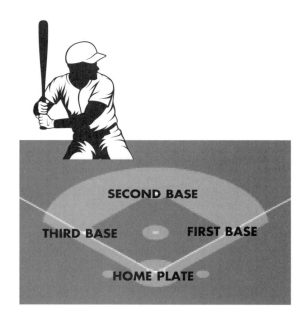

SECOND BASE

THIRD BASE   FIRST BASE

HOME PLATE

- A player can advance past first base in the following situations:
    - A batter hits the pitched ball "away from" the opposing players long enough for him to advance past first base to second base, third base or home plate without being tagged out by the ball in a fielder's hand (or a fielder's glove that contains the ball).
        1. For the batter to be out at first base, a fielder who has possession of the ball must only *touch first base* before the batter does, because the batter is forced to run to first (called a FORCE OUT).
        2. At second, third or home plate, a fielder must *touch the batter* with the ball (or with his glove containing the ball) to get him out, since the batter is not forced to run to those bases.
    - The batter hits a pitched ball that touches the ground (called a GROUNDER or GROUND BALL), and a RUNNER (a previous batter who reached first base successfully) reaches second base before an opposing player holding the ball touches that base or tags out the runner.
    - When a pitched ball is not hit by a batter and the runner on first base makes it to second base before being tagged by an opposing player.
        1. If the runner was safe at second base because the pitched ball could not have been caught by the catcher (due to the pitcher's mistake), it is called a WILD PITCH.
        2. If the runner is safe at second because the catcher missed the ball (his fault), it is called a PASSED BALL.
        3. If the runner is safe at second because the catcher did not even try to throw him out (usually due to a lopsided game score), it is attributed to CATCHER'S INDIFFERENCE.
        4. Otherwise, the runner who arrived at second base is credited with a STOLEN BASE.

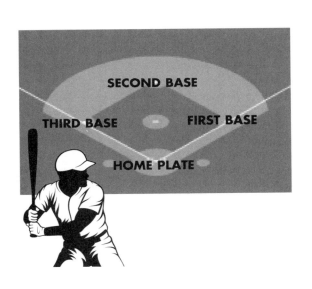

SECOND BASE

THIRD BASE

FIRST BASE

HOME PLATE

- When a subsequent batter hits a pitched ball (in the air) that is caught by an opposing player and the runner on first base arrives at second base before an opposing player touches him with the ball. In this situation, the runner cannot leave first base until the ball has been caught. A runner who advances in this manner is said to have run after TAGGING UP.

- The runner on first base is "automatically awarded" second base when:

    1. The batter gets "walked" (earning a base on balls).

    2. The batter is hit by a pitch.

    3. There is catcher's interference with the batter.

    4. The pitcher BALKS (illegally deceiving the runner) while his foot is on the rubber part of the pitcher's mound.

        a. The pitcher fakes a throw to first base when there is a runner at that base. (He is ALLOWED to fake a throw to second or third base.)

        b. The pitcher fails to, first, step in the direction of his throw to a base in an attempt to PICK OFF a runner.

        c. The pitcher does not come to a "full stop" when pitching from a SET POSITION (discussed in detail later).

- The rules that apply for a runner to advance past first base also apply for a runner to advance past second base and third base toward home plate.

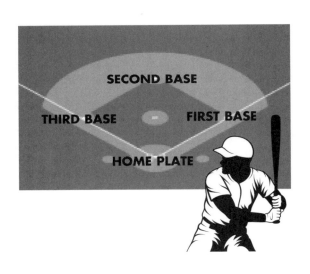

SECOND BASE

THIRD BASE   FIRST BASE

HOME PLATE

How can a player "fail"? How does he make an out?

- ◆ The batter hits a pitched ball that is caught in the air (before it hits the ground) by an opposing player.

- ◆ The batter hits a ground ball and fails to arrive at first base before an opposing player touches the base with the ball in his possession by:

  - – Catching the ball when another teammate throws it to him.

  - – Fielding the ground ball himself, called UNASSISTED.

- ◆ The batter hits a pitched ball (not caught by an opposing player), and is then tagged with the ball while he is in between (not touching) bases. An exception: if the batter overruns first base, he cannot be tagged out unless he is judged to have "made a move toward" second base.

- ◆ A runner fails to arrive at a base (that he was forced to advance to) before an opposing player touches that base with the ball in his possession. Such a runner is always forced to advance to the next base when a batted ball hits the ground and every base behind him is "occupied" by a teammate. For example, when there are runners at first and third base, only the runner at third is not forced to advance (since there is not a runner on second base).

- ◆ A runner is tagged with the ball while not touching one of the bases.

- ◆ A batter STRIKES OUT. This is a combination of any three of the following occurrences (called strikes):

  - – A batter swings the bat and misses a pitched ball.

  - – A batter does not swing at a pitched ball that passes through the strike zone. This is a CALLED STRIKE.

  - – A batter (who has less than two strikes) hits the ball, but it goes FOUL. A foul ball is a batted ball that:

    1. Passes outside of first or third base on the ground.

    2. Ends up, or is touched by a player, outside of either foul line (which extend from home plate to the outfield fence) *before* reaching first or third base.

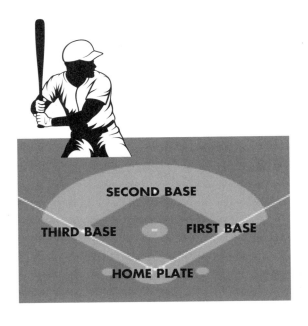

SECOND BASE

THIRD BASE   FIRST BASE

HOME PLATE

3. Hits the ground outside of either foul line *after* passing first or third base. When a ball is hit over the fence in the air, "foul poles" aligned with each foul line at the outfield fence help determine if a ball is fair or foul.

◆ When a batter who already has two strikes BUNTS the ball foul, it is also ruled a strikeout. A bunt is a pitched ball that is intentionally tapped lightly by a hitter's bat.

◆ When a batted ball is caught in the air by an opposing player, and a base runner fails to touch his original base (called TAGGING UP) before an opposing player with the ball in his possession touches that base, the base runner is out.

◆ A runner is hit by a batted ball before any opposing player touches it. This does not happen very often.

Some special rules:

◆ When a batter has two strikes and hits a foul ball, it is not a strikeout, and the batter continues his at bat.

◆ When a batted ball in foul territory is not caught before it touches the ground, all base runners must return to their original bases before the next pitch can be made.

◆ Even if a runner touches home plate *before* the third out is made (and that out was a force out), the run does *not* count. Suppose a runner is on third base with two outs. The batter hits a ground ball to the first baseman, who then touches first base before the batter does resulting in the third out. Even if the runner from third had touched home plate before the force out at first, the run does not count.

◆ A batter can try to reach first base on a third strike if the catcher misses the ball. However, when first base is occupied and there are less than two outs, the batter is automatically out. The reason for this exception is to prevent the catcher from getting two outs by intentionally dropping a third strike, throwing the ball to second base to force that runner out and then having the ball thrown on to first to get the batter.

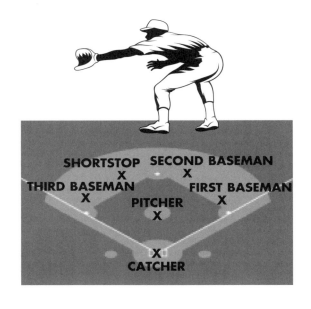

SHORTSTOP   SECOND BASEMAN
X   X
THIRD BASEMAN   FIRST BASEMAN
X   X
PITCHER
X

X
CATCHER

PLAYERS IN THE FIELD (DEFENSE)

Infielders:

- ◆ First baseman
    - – Responsible for fielding balls hit to him and catching throws from infield teammates (who field ground balls) in order to force out the batters.
    - – May be either right-handed or left-handed.
    - – Requires minimal running and throwing. Older players sometimes end their careers at this position. Some famous players who made this transition include Willie Mays, Mickey Mantle, Pete Rose, and Henry Aaron.
- ◆ Second baseman
    - – Responsible for fielding balls hit to him.
    - – With a runner on first base, he is responsible for COVERING (standing near) second base when a ground ball has been hit to the left side of the infield.
    - – Responsible for covering first base when a batter bunts the ball to try to advance a runner.
    - – Throws right-handed because:
        1. It is easier to field the ground balls hit to his right side and throw to first base. (A player who throws left-handed would have a hard time completing a quick and accurate throw to first base after fielding the ball hit to his right. TRY IT!)
        2. When covering second base, it is easier to throw to first base after catching the ball from another fielder. TRY THIS, TOO!
    - – Doesn't have to possess a strong throwing arm, since he is so close to first base.
- ◆ Shortstop
    - – Responsible for fielding balls hit to him.
    - – With a runner on first base, he is responsible for covering second base when a ground ball is hit to the right side of the infield.

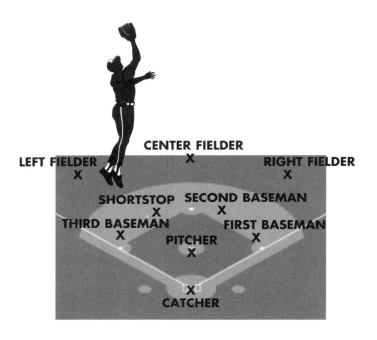

CENTER FIELDER
X

LEFT FIELDER
X

RIGHT FIELDER
X

SHORTSTOP   SECOND BASEMAN
X   X

THIRD BASEMAN   FIRST BASEMAN
X   X

PITCHER
X

X
CATCHER

- Usually the best infielder, since most ground balls are hit to him.

- In most cases, has the strongest throwing arm of all the infielders because he often throws to first base from the farthest distance away.

- Throws right-handed because it is easier to field ground balls that are hit to his right side and throw to first base.

◆ Third baseman

- Responsible for fielding balls hit to him and for covering third base.

- Must be especially alert, because many balls are hit to him sharply. In fact, third base is sometimes called the "HOT CORNER" for that reason.

- Throws right-handed because it is easier to field ground balls to his right side and throw to first base.

Outfielders:

◆ Left fielder

- Usually has the weakest arm, since his throws are not as long as those of the other two outfielders.

- He rarely has to make the long throw to first base.

◆ Center fielder

- Because he has more area to cover, he is likely to be the fastest outfielder.

- Usually the best fielding outfielder, since he is involved in the most plays.

◆ Right fielder

- Usually has the strongest throwing arm of the outfielders.

- Must be able to make the long throws to third base when necessary.

One of the most famous pitchers in
the history of baseball was Cy Young.
He got his nickname when he was
auditioning for a team in Ohio during
the late 1880s. A couple of his practice throws went over his catcher's
head and crashed into the wooden
seats, sending people scattering.
Those in attendance compared him
to a cyclone because of "the damage
he could cause." So, they shortened it
to Cy and the name stuck. He went
on to win 511 games in his career
from 1890 to 1911. Each year the
best pitcher in each league, as
voted by the media, is given the
"Cy Young" award.

THE BATTERY (pitcher and catcher):

- ◆ Pitcher
    - – Initiates the action of each play by throwing the ball toward home plate where the batter is prepared to hit it with his bat.
    - – Needs to have a strong throwing arm. Many pitchers can throw a ball 90–100 miles per hour.
    - – Must have CONTROL (accuracy when throwing the ball in the strike zone).
    - – Usually not a very good batter.
        1. Pitchers spend most of their practice time on pitching, not hitting.
        2. For more excitement, teams in the American League of Major League Baseball use an extra batter (referred to as a DESIGNATED HITTER) who bats instead of the pitcher.
    - – Responsible for covering first base when a ground ball is hit to the first baseman.
    - – There are two categories of pitchers:
        1. Starting pitchers
            a. The one who begins the game.
            b. Usually pitches every fifth day.
            c. Considered part of the team's pitching ROTATION of starting pitchers.
        2. Relief pitchers
            a. Those who do not begin the game.
            b. Could pitch nearly every day, since they only pitch a few innings (at the most) during appearances.
            c. Most teams now have a specialist, called the CLOSER, who is called upon to pitch primarily in the ninth inning, when his team is ahead by a slim margin.

On April 3, 1931, the New York Yankees were in Chattanooga, Tennessee, for an exhibition game against the Chattanooga Lookouts, a minor league team of players aspiring to play one day in the major leagues. The Lookouts put a relief pitcher in the game, Jackie Mitchell, to face two of baseball's greatest players— Babe Ruth and Lou Gehrig— and struck them both out. Why was that unusual? Because Jackie Mitchell was a seventeen-year-old girl who was never allowed to play again because of her gender. She always claimed those strikeouts were legitimate and that nobody could hit her excellent curveball.

◆ Catcher:

- Wears a mask, chest protector, shin guards, and other safety equipment while crouched behind the batter. Since the catcher's position is so dangerous, his equipment is jokingly referred to as the TOOLS OF IGNORANCE.

- Receives the ball from the pitcher, unless the batter hits it.

- Has a very strong arm in order to throw out runners attempting to steal bases.

- Must be tough and durable.

  1. There are often collisions at home plate with base runners attempting to score.

  2. Frequently gets hit by foul balls that just nick the bat, called FOUL TIPS.

- Gives signals to the pitcher that tell what types of pitches to throw to the batters.

  1. FASTBALL — Thrown extremely hard, usually 85–95 mph.

  2. CURVEBALL — Not thrown as hard as a fastball, it follows a sharp, curved path as it reaches the batter.

  3. SLIDER — In between a fastball and a curveball in terms of speed and movement.

  4. SPLIT-FINGER FASTBALL — Initially appears to be a fastball, but moves sharply down as it reaches the batter.

  5. CHANGE-UP (or LET-UP) — A slower fastball meant to deceive the hitter.

  6. KNUCKLE BALL — Thrown without normal spin, air currents make the ball's flight unpredictable. Because of the wacky movement of this pitch, the catcher will sometimes wear an oversized glove when catching a knuckle ball pitcher.

The New York Yankees, in 1929, were the first team to wear uniform numbers on a consistent basis. The players were assigned numbers according to their position in the batting order. Babe Ruth, the number three hitter, wore that number on the back of his shirt.

THE PLAYERS AT BAT (OFFENSE)

The BATTING ORDER (or LINEUP):

- ◆ First Hitter (called LEADOFF)
    - – Good speed.
    - – Not a lot of home run (POWER) potential.
    - – Often the shortest player in the lineup, making him more difficult to pitch to. This gives him a better chance to get on base (due to walks) to set up scoring opportunities.

- ◆ Second Hitter
    - – Good bunter.
    - – Not a lot of power.

- ◆ Third Hitter
    - – Usually the best hitter in terms of BATTING AVERAGE (number of base hits per times at bat).
    - – A good power hitter.

- ◆ Fourth Hitter (CLEANUP) — Most likely to hit a home run.

- ◆ Fifth Hitter — Similar to the characteristics of the third hitter.

- ◆ Sixth Hitter — Similar to the characteristics of the second hitter.

- ◆ Seventh Hitter — A better fielder than hitter.

- ◆ Eighth Hitter — Similar to the characteristics of the seventh hitter.

- ◆ Ninth Hitter — The pitcher almost always bats in this position in the lineup (except in the American League of Major League Baseball which uses a DESIGNATED HITTER instead of letting the pitcher bat).

The effect of substitutions and defensive changes on the batting order:

- ◆ Once a player is replaced by a substitute player and leaves the game, he cannot reenter the game at a later time. This rule makes a manager's substitution decisions especially important.

- ◆ If a player changes fielding positions (e.g. moving from right field to center field), he must still bat in his original spot in the order.

Henry Aaron is the all-time home run leader with 755 during his career. He broke the record previously held by Babe Ruth, who hit 714 home runs.

TERMS AND DEFINITIONS

BASE HIT (or HIT) — A single, double, triple, or home run.

- ◆ SINGLE — When a batter hits the ball and reaches first base safely (through no fault of a fielder).

- ◆ DOUBLE — When a batter hits the ball and reaches second base safely (through no fault of a fielder). If a batter hits a ball that bounces over the outfield fence, it is a GROUND RULE DOUBLE, and all runners are allowed to advance two bases.

- ◆ TRIPLE — When a batter hits the ball and reaches third base safely (through no fault of a fielder).

- ◆ HOME RUN — When a batter hits the ball and reaches home plate safely (through no fault of a fielder) by either:
    - – Hitting the ball in the air over the outfield fence.
    - – Hitting the ball within the playing field and advancing to home plate before being tagged out (called an INSIDE THE PARK HOME RUN).

Types of batted balls caught in the air for outs:

- ◆ FLY OUT — A ball hit high in the air and caught by an outfielder.

- ◆ POP OUT — A ball hit high in the air and caught by an infielder, catcher or pitcher.

- ◆ LINE OUT — A ball hit hard in a straight line and caught by an infielder, outfielder or pitcher.

For seven straight years, from 1958 to 1964, Dick Stuart led the major leagues or was tied for the lead in the number of errors by a first baseman. Stuart was affectionately called "Dr. Strangeglove" throughout his career. He even drove around in a car that had a license plate "E-3" (the scoring when an error is charged to the first baseman). Stuart once said, "One night in Pittsburgh, thirty thousand fans gave me a standing ovation when I caught a hot-dog wrapper on the fly."

Other Terms:

- ◆ ERROR — A fielder's wild throw or misplay of a batted ball that allows a batter (or runner) to advance to a base or bases. If a fielder fails to catch an "easy" foul pop or fly (which allows a batter to continue his time at bat), it is also considered an error.

- ◆ SLIDING — When a runner intentionally falls to the ground as he approaches a base. Runners slide because it is:

    - A good way to come to a stop precisely at a base after running full speed.

    - A way to avoid being tagged out by a fielder. You rarely see a slide at first base, because a batter is allowed to overrun first, and (since it is a force play) there is no tag to avoid.

- ◆ PUTOUT — Credit given to the last player to have possession of the ball when a batter or runner makes an out. The first baseman and catcher usually have the most putouts in a game, since most outs occur at first base and at home plate (by strikeouts).

- ◆ ASSIST — Credit given to the player who helped achieve a putout. Some examples of players earning an assist are:

    - An infielder who fields a ground ball and throws to first base to force out the batter.

    - An outfielder who picks up a ground ball and throws it to an infielder or catcher who tags out a runner.

- ◆ DOUBLE PLAY (or DP) — When two players are called out on one continuing play.

    - Most common double play: a runner is on first base, and a batter hits a ground ball to the shortstop, who throws it to the second baseman (who is touching second base with his foot to force out a runner) and who then throws the ball to the first baseman to force out the batter.

    - Other names for a double play are TWIN KILLING and PITCHER'S BEST FRIEND.

- ◆ TRIPLE PLAY — When three players are called out on one continuing play. A very rare occurrence.

On May 29, 1959, Harvey Haddix pitched the greatest game ever by a losing pitcher. He had a perfect game through 12 innings, retiring all 36 batters (12 X 3). Unfortunately, his Pittsburgh Pirates also failed to score, so the game continued to the 13th inning. Haddix's third baseman bobbled a ground ball for an error, ending the perfect game, but the no-hitter was still intact. However, later in the inning, an opposing player hit a home run causing Haddix to lose both the no-hitter and the game.

- ◆ INFIELD FLY RULE — In certain circumstances, when a batter hits a pop fly to an infielder, *the batter is automatically called out* (even if the infielder fails to catch the ball). This rule prevents the infielders from benefitting by intentionally dropping a pop fly.
    - For the infield fly rule to be in effect, there must be:
        1. Fewer than two outs in the inning.
        2. Runners on first and second; or first, second and third (BASES LOADED).
    - The infield fly rule is necessary, because:
        1. On an infield pop fly (with less than two outs), base runners normally remain near their original bases to avoid making additional outs after the catch.
        2. Ordinarily, if the pop fly is dropped, the base runners would be forced to attempt to advance to the next base. The fielders could then easily get a double or triple play by picking up the dropped ball and throwing it to bases to which the runners were forced to go. With the infield fly rule, the batter is automatically out, so the runners on base are not forced to advance.
- ◆ The COUNT — The current number of balls and strikes on a hitter. When reciting the count, the number of balls precedes the number of strikes. Examples:
    - If the first two pitches to a batter are strikes, the count is no balls, 2 strikes (Ø and 2).
    - If the first four pitches result in 1 strike and 3 balls, the count is 3 balls, 1 strike (3 and 1).
    - FULL COUNT: 3 balls, 2 strikes (3 and 2).
    - Count is even: 1 ball and 1 strike (1 and 1), or 2 balls and 2 strikes (2 and 2).
- ◆ NO-HITTER — When a team allows no base hits to the opposing team during the game; a rare feat.
- ◆ PERFECT GAME — When a team allows absolutely no base runners to the opposing team during the game; a very rare accomplishment.

Umpires often receive verbal abuse from players during the game. Former pitcher Dizzy Dean once questioned a call made by umpire George Barr, who then ignored the pitcher. Dean was upset that he did not get any response to his protest. Barr maintained that he had "shaken his head." Dean said that he had "not heard anything rattle."

- ◆ COMPLETE GAME — When a starting pitcher pitches the entire game (without the assistance of a relief pitcher).

- ◆ SHUTOUT — When a team does not allow the opposing team to score any runs during the game.

- ◆ BENCH — Substitute players; those who did not start the game and generally sit on "the bench."

- ◆ DUGOUT — Two covered areas facing first and third base where each team's players sit when they are not actually batting, on base or fielding.

- ◆ BULLPEN — Areas for each team behind the right field and left field foul lines or behind the right field and left field fences where players (usually relief pitchers) practice throwing (called WARMING UP) before entering the game. The starting pitchers also warm up there before the game.

- ◆ CLUBHOUSE — The "locker rooms" usually connected to the dugouts where players shower and dress.

- ◆ UMPIRES — The four officials who arbitrate the proceedings of a game.

- ◆ MANAGER — The "head coach" who directs his team's actions during a game.

- ◆ COACHES — The manager's assistants.
  - When a team is batting, a coach stands in each of two designated areas called COACHES BOXES (one by first base and another by third base) to relay game strategy to the batter and runners by using prearranged secret hand signals.
  - When a pitched ball is hit, the coaches become "extra eyes" for the batter and base runners, signaling for them to either keep running or stop at certain bases.

LeRoy "Satchel" Paige, the oldest player ever to play in the major leagues (at age 59), was known for his excellent pitching control. During practice, he used to show off his pinpoint throwing accuracy by consistently putting his pitches exactly over the top of a soft drink bottle.

COMMON OFFENSIVE STRATEGIES

TAKING THE PITCH — In certain situations (e.g., if the count is 3 balls and no strikes), it is a given that most hitters will almost never swing at the next pitch.

- ◆ The batter does not want to jeopardize a potential walk by being tempted to swing at a pitch outside of the strike zone that would (in this example) have been ball four.

- ◆ The pressure is on the pitcher to throw a strike or give up the base on balls.

- ◆ Occasionally, the best hitters (usually the third, fourth and fifth hitters in the order) will swing in this situation (referred to as SWINGING AWAY or HAVING THE GREEN LIGHT).

    - – Most pitchers throw a fastball in this situation, because it is their most accurate pitch. A batter is aware of this, and it is easier for him to hit the pitch that he is anticipating.

    - – Hitting a "good pitch" may produce a double, triple or home run instead of only reaching first base on the walk.

SACRIFICE BUNT — A batter taps a pitched ball with his loosely held bat (so that the ball will travel only a few yards) in order to advance a runner to the next base. Since the batter is usually put out at first base, he is said to have "sacrificed" his time at bat.

- ◆ The most common situations for a sacrifice bunt are when:

    - – There are no outs, and a runner is on first base. The batter's goal is to move the runner to second base (called SCORING POSITION), where he can probably score if a subsequent batter hits a single. (Third base is also scoring position, since a runner on third will almost always score if an upcoming batter hits a single.)

    - – There are no outs, and runners are on both first and second base. The batter's goal is to move the runners to second and third base, respectively.

In 1962, when San Francisco Giants Manager Alvin Dark first saw his pitcher Gaylord Perry swing a bat, he said, "A man will land on the moon before Gaylord will hit a home run in the big leagues." On July 20, 1969, Gaylord Perry did hit his first major league home run over the center field fence in a 7-3 win over the Los Angeles Dodgers. Dark was right by 40 minutes. That was the day Neil Armstrong and Buzz Aldrin made their historic landing on the moon.

1. Moving the runner to third provides an opportunity for him to score on any of the following:

   a. SACRIFICE FLY: hit to an outfielder. The runner on third base can tag up and advance to home plate once the outfielder catches the ball. Note that a runner can tag up and advance even if the fly ball that is caught is a foul ball.

   b. WILD PITCH: thrown by the pitcher.

   c. PASSED BALL: missed by the catcher.

   d. ERROR: by a fielder.

   e. BASE HIT: by a batter.

   f. GROUND OUT: by a batter.

- A pitcher bats. (He might also be asked to sacrifice bunt when there is one out). Reasons include:

   1. The pitcher is usually a poor hitter. Because he will probably make an out anyway, he may as well do it in a way (by bunting) that could advance the runner(s).

   2. To avoid hitting a ground ball that might result in a double play.

- ◆ Very rarely will a team sacrifice bunt if it is behind by three or more runs, because:

   - A sacrifice bunt is generally used when a team needs only one or two runs to either tie or go ahead of the other team.

   - A team that is three or more runs behind may not want to give up a valuable out (even if the runner does score), and still be losing by a significant margin.

Can you imagine a baseball player never needing a bat or glove during his career? Herb Washington, a former track star at Michigan State University (the alma mater of my mom, by the way), was such a player. In 1974 and 1975, the Oakland Athletics used Washington strictly as a pinch runner, stealing 31 bases in 48 attempts. He also scored 33 runs during those two seasons, after which this "experiment" ended.

STEALING (A BASE) — At his own risk, a base runner advances to the next base during a pitched ball or strike to a batter. This strategy is most common when there is a fast runner on first, regardless of how many outs, with the team not more than one run behind.

- ◆ Stealing helps a team in the following ways:
    - – Moves a runner into scoring position without sacrificing an out.
    - – By already having the runner at second base, a double play can be avoided (if the next batter hits a ground ball to an infielder).
- ◆ It is less common for a runner to steal third base, because:
    - – The catcher's throw to third is shorter than his throw to second, so there is a greater likelihood of the runner being tagged out at third.
    - – With two outs, the additional benefit of being on third base rather than on second may not be worth the risk of making the third (final) out of the inning. Either way, the runner would be in scoring position.

PINCH RUNNER — A player from the bench enters the game to run in place of a teammate on base. A pinch runner is typically used in the following situations:

- ◆ To increase the chance of a successful stolen base, a manager may substitute a faster player for the runner on first base.
- ◆ If a slow runner is on third base, and there are less than two outs, a pinch runner will have a better chance of scoring on a sacrifice fly.
- ◆ If there is a slow runner on second base, a pinch runner will have a better chance of scoring on a single that is hit to the outfield.
- ◆ A pinch runner is primarily used in the later innings of a game, because the manager does not want to replace a starting player (who will not be allowed to return) early in the game for the mere chance of scoring one run.

Bill Veeck, the former owner of the old St. Louis Browns, showed the baseball world why he was an unusual character. On August 18, 1951, he ordered his manager Zack Taylor to use a pinch hitter, 3-foot-10-inch-tall Eddie Gaedel. Of course, he walked on four straight pitches because of his small strike zone. Gaedel was immediately substituted for by a pinch runner and greeted by the crowd with a rousing ovation. It was Gaedel's last game, as midgets were banned thereafter by baseball's management.

PLAYING THE PERCENTAGES — Substitution of a batter or pitcher (by a team's manager), according to whether the player bats or pitches right-handed or left-handed. Statistics show that batters are usually more successful when hitting "opposite" from the way a pitcher pitches, and pitchers do better when they pitch from the "same side." (A handy way to remember "who prefers what" is by referring to it as the *B-O-P-S* principle — that is, *Batter: Opposite; Pitcher: Same.*)

- It is easier for a right-handed batter to hit a pitch from a left-handed pitcher, and for a left-handed batter to hit a pitch from a right-handed pitcher.

  - The batter is better able to see the ball when the pitcher releases it on the *opposite* side of home plate from where the batter is standing.

  - A curveball, or slider, moves *toward* the batter, rather than darting away from him in the case of a "same-handed" pitcher.

- The best hitters are often able to overcome the percentages and succeed no matter who is pitching.

- A batter who is able to bat either right-handed or left-handed (called a SWITCH HITTER) always has the percentages in his favor, since he can bat right-handed if a left-handed pitcher is throwing, or left-handed if facing a right-handed pitcher.

PINCH HITTER — A player from the bench enters the game (when more runs are needed) to bat in the place of a teammate who was scheduled to hit.

- A pinch hitter is used primarily when the pitcher, or another poor hitter, is scheduled to bat.

- A pinch hitter is also used when "playing the percentages." If a left-handed pitcher is pitching, and a left-handed batter is scheduled to hit, a manager might send up a right-handed pinch hitter instead.

  - The opposing manager in the situation above might counter that move by bringing in a right-handed relief pitcher to regain the advantage.

  - Then, the manager of the team at bat might use a left-handed batter to pinch hit for his right-handed pinch hitter.

The hit and run is widely believed to have been invented in the mid-1890s by John McGraw and Willie Keeler of the Baltimore Orioles—a team so renowned for their original, deceptive plays that opposing owners had to enact new rules to counteract them. The term emerged in the mainstream in the 1930s to describe automobile accidents in which damage was caused by a driver who then left the scene. Today, a "hit and run" can describe anything which happens quickly.

- The "chess match" stops there, because (according to the rules) a relief pitcher must pitch to at least one batter before being removed from the game.

    1. A pinch hitter, however, does *not* have to bat before being removed from the game.

    2. Therefore, the offensive team can always have the percentages in its favor (if they are willing to "spend" the players).

PLATOONING — Two players sharing a fielding position on the team because they hit from opposite sides of the plate.

- ◆ A right-handed hitter starts at the platooned position when the opposing team starts a left-handed pitcher.

- ◆ A left-handed hitter starts at the platooned position when the opposing team starts a right-handed pitcher.

HIT AND RUN — A runner on first attempts to steal second base, while the batter hits the ball in the area vacated by the second baseman (or shortstop) who has moved to cover second base against the steal attempt.

- ◆ The result of a successful hit and run play is runners on first and third for the team at bat.

- ◆ When a right-handed batter is up, the second baseman will usually cover second on a steal, because right-handed batters normally hit the ball to the left side of the field. On a hit and run, the batter aims to hit the ball to the right side of the field (in the area vacated by the second baseman).

- ◆ When a left-handed batter is up, the shortstop will usually cover second base on a steal, because left-handed batters normally hit the ball to the right side of the field. On a hit and run, the batter aims to hit the ball to the left side of the field (in the area vacated by the shortstop).

- ◆ If the batter swings and misses, the hit and run play becomes an attempted steal.

One of the most exciting plays in baseball because of its "all or nothing" dimension (it almost always results in an easy score or a sure out), the suicide squeeze has been practiced nearly 100 years. One version says Joel Yeager introduced it to the Major Leagues in 1898 and another maintains Clark Griffith implemented it in 1904.

HIT TO THE RIGHT SIDE — When there is a runner on second with no outs, many batters will try to hit the ball to the right side of the field.

- Since third base is a long throw from where the second baseman or first baseman fields a ground ball, the fielder will usually ignore the runner in order to get the batter out at first base.

- The objective is to move the runner to third base where he can easily score on a sacrifice fly.

- This strategy might be used instead of a bunt, because a ball hit to the right side has a better chance of resulting in a base hit. The batter would then reach base safely, while the runner from second base could probably score.

- A hit to the right side is easier for left-handed hitters, because most of them naturally hit to the right side of the field. A hit to the right side for right-handed batters is not natural for them, making it even more of an accomplishment.

- A player who successfully hits to the right side, even if he makes an out for himself at first, will be congratulated by fellow teammates. Watch for it at the next game!

SQUEEZE PLAY — A bunt designed to score a runner from third base (when there are fewer than two outs).

- Suicide Squeeze— As the pitcher delivers the ball to the batter, the runner on third runs toward home plate. The batter then bunts the ball on the ground. Since the runner had a head start, he usually scores easily, leaving the fielder with a single option: to try to get the batter out at first base.

    - The play can be "suicide" for the runner if the batter misses the ball while attempting to bunt. The catcher would then be waiting at home plate to easily tag the runner out.

Everybody has an off-day, but Joe DiMaggio didn't have one for 56 straight games. DiMaggio, known as the "Yankee Clipper," got a base hit in 56 games in a row while playing for the New York Yankees in 1941. The closest anyone has come to that record was 44 straight games by Pete Rose in 1978. This is a record that may never be broken.

- The play can also be "suicide" if the batter pops up the ball to a fielder who catches it. Remember, after a batted ball is caught in the air, a runner is forced to touch his original base. Therefore, if a fielder touches third base with the ball in his possession before the runner arrives there (which is likely because the runner is probably halfway to home plate when the bunt was attempted) the runner is out. The end result is a costly double play.

◆ SAFETY SQUEEZE — Similar to the suicide squeeze, except the runner on third does not dash toward home unless the batter has bunted the ball on the ground.

   - Requires a faster runner, since his start toward home plate begins later than with a suicide squeeze.

   - Requires a better bunt than with a suicide squeeze, because it must elude a fielder long enough for the runner to beat the short throw to home plate.

START THE MERRY-GO-ROUND — Runners (in a bases-loaded situation) seeking an advantage by starting to run as the pitcher delivers the ball to home plate. The effect of the three runners "moving on the pitch" is said to resemble the circular motion of a merry-go-round. This only happens when the count to the batter is 3 balls, 2 strikes and there are 2 out.

◆ There is no risk to the runners, because if the batter:

   - Strikes out, grounds out or flies out, the inning will be over anyway.

   - Walks, then the runners are awarded the next base anyway.

   - Gets a base hit, the runners should reach the next base (or additional bases) safely.

Mel Ott, a former player for the Giants, also managed the team later in his career. He had a rule that his pitchers were to never throw a strike when they had an 0 and 2 count on a hitter. Ott insisted that the pitchers "waste a pitch" in that situation, or they would be fined $500. One of Ott's younger pitchers once had an 0 and 2 count on a hitter and mistakenly threw a called strike three that just nipped the outside corner of the plate. Hoping to avoid the fine, the pitcher protested vehemently that it was a ball. A pitcher arguing with an umpire to change a call from a strike to a ball is surely not an ordinary situation.

COMMON DEFENSIVE STRATEGIES

INTENTIONAL WALK — A pitcher purposely throws four balls far enough outside so that the batter cannot hit the ball, putting him on first base with a walk. This is done when:

◆ There is a runner on any base other than first, with less than two out. An intentional walk creates a situation where a subsequent batter might hit into a double play.

◆ The pitcher does not have the "percentages" advantage over the current batter (the righty/lefty scenario) but *does* have the advantage against the next batter. An intentional walk will allow the pitcher to pitch to that next batter.

PITCHOUT — A ball purposely pitched away from the batter to make it easier for the catcher to throw out a base runner. A pitchout is used when a team thinks that the runner will be attempting to steal a base.

◆ The downside risk is that if a pitchout results in a ball, it is one pitch closer to a walk.

◆ A pitchout is rarely thrown when there are already two balls on a batter.

WASTE A PITCH — A pitch deliberately thrown out of the strike zone (when the count is 0 and 2 or 1 and 2) to entice an anxious batter to swing at a bad pitch.

INFIELD IN — During a close game with a runner on third, the infielders are told to move in closer than usual to enable them to prevent an important run from scoring on a ground ball.

◆ If an infielder fields a ground ball, he will have a shorter throw to home plate in an attempt to throw out a runner.

◆ The drawbacks to this defensive alignment are:

– The infielders don't have as much time to react to a hard-hit ground ball.

Some ballparks have used golf carts to drive relief pitchers who enter the game from the bullpen to the pitcher's mound. Mike Flanagan, a pitcher with the Baltimore Orioles, once said, "I could never play in New York. The first time I came into a game there and got into the bullpen car, they told me to lock the doors."

– There is more room in the outfield for a pop fly to drop safely.

PLAYING THE PERCENTAGES — Changing pitchers so that a right-handed pitcher faces a right-handed hitter or a left-handed pitcher throws against a left-handed hitter. Remember *B-O-P-S* (*Batter: Opposite; Pitcher: Same*).

◆ Forces an opposing manager to think about replacing the scheduled hitter with a pinch hitter who will again give his team the "percentages" advantage.

◆ The opposing manager probably won't make that move if one of his best hitters is scheduled to bat. Therefore, the new pitcher will keep the advantage from a percentage standpoint.

DOUBLE SWITCH — A manager brings in a relief pitcher and substitutes a player at another position at the same time.

◆ When a pitcher is scheduled to bat in the next inning, the manager doesn't want to use a pinch hitter for the relief pitcher, because still another pitcher would have to be used in the following inning.

◆ Therefore, the new "other player" who also entered the game, bats in the prior pitcher's spot in the batting order (usually ninth). The new relief pitcher bats in the spot of the replaced "other player" (who usually made the last out in the previous inning).

◆ This tactic delays the time when the new relief pitcher will be scheduled to bat and allows a good relief pitcher to stay in the game longer.

◆ A double switch is not used in the American League of Major League Baseball. The pitcher does not bat because of the designated hitter.

Former pitcher Dave LaPoint, when asked what it felt like after losing 25 pounds: "I felt the difference when I went into the set position and did not have anything to rest my hands on."

(Pitching from a) SET POSITION versus a FULL WINDUP
— The classic pitching style is called a FULL WINDUP, with both hands lifted over the pitcher's head. He then brings his hands down and steps toward the plate while throwing the baseball. The rules state that once a windup is started, it cannot be stopped or a balk is called, automatically advancing each runner one base. Since the windup delivery is so time-consuming, it would be easy for a base runner to steal during the pitch. Therefore, when a runner is on base, a pitcher delivers the ball from a SET POSITION.

- The pitcher stands sideways, with one foot touching the rubber plate on the pitcher's mound. He then takes a half step away from home plate while bringing both hands together for a pause. After this mandatory halt, the pitcher either throws to a base in an attempt to PICK OFF a runner, or throws the pitch to the plate.

- When there is a runner on third base, a pitcher might still choose to go to a full windup to put more power into the pitch. There is very little risk of the runner on third stealing home during a windup, because the catcher would be waiting with the ball in his hand for the runner. Only if the runner is extremely fast could he beat a pitcher's throw from a windup to home plate.

- Some relief pitchers are so accustomed to entering a game with runners on base and pitching from a set position that they pitch from the set position even when there are no runners on base.

Author Pat Conroy once said, "Baseball fans love numbers. They love to swirl them around their mouths like Bordeaux wine."

SCORING AND STATISTICS

KEEPING SCORE with a scorecard.

- ◆ Helpful in keeping track of what has taken place during the game.
- ◆ The scorecard is usually found in the middle of the game program sold at the ballpark.
- ◆ The scorecard has spaces to fill in the lineups and positions of the players on each team.

Each player's position is assigned a number. (The abbreviation for each position is also listed.)

- ◆ Pitcher (p) = 1
- ◆ Catcher (c) = 2
- ◆ First baseman (1b) = 3
- ◆ Second baseman (2b) = 4
- ◆ Third baseman (3b) = 5
- ◆ Shortstop (ss) = 6
- ◆ Left fielder (lf) = 7
- ◆ Center fielder (cf) = 8
- ◆ Right fielder (rf) = 9

Common scorecard abbreviations show the action that has taken place in the game.

- ◆ BB = Base on Balls
- ◆ Bk = Balk
- ◆ E = Error
- ◆ FC = FIELDER'S CHOICE
  - – A fielder catches a ground ball and tries to get a runner out instead of the batter.
  - – The batter does reach first base safely, but is not given credit for a base hit.
- ◆ HBP = Hit by Pitch

The letter K is the abbreviation used for strikeout in baseball scoring and statistics. Some historians believe that New York baseball writer M. J. Kelly chose "K" because it was the last letter of the word "struck." Others believe he chose K because it is the first letter of his last name. He couldn't use "S" because that was already taken to stand for "sacrifice."

- ◆ K or SO = Strikeout (a "backward K" is a Called Strikeout)
- ◆ PB = Passed Ball
- ◆ SB = Stolen Base
- ◆ CS = Caught Stealing
- ◆ S = Sacrifice Bunt
- ◆ SF = Sacrifice Fly
- ◆ WP = Wild Pitch
- ◆ L = Lined Out
- ◆ P = Popped Out
- ◆ F = Flied Out
- ◆ lB = Single
- ◆ 2B = Double
- ◆ 3B = Triple
- ◆ HR = Home Run
- ◆ U = Unassisted
- ◆ CI = Catcher's Interference

In each box on the scorecard, two different items are recorded for each batter who reaches base safely:

- ◆ What the player did during his time at bat.
- ◆ His progress around the bases until he either scores or the inning is over.
  - – When a batter reaches first base, draw the bottom right side of a diamond (simulating the batter's path from home to first.) Next to that line, describe how he advanced to first base using the appropriate scorecard abbreviation. For example a batter who singled would be reflected in the scorecard as:

    /*1B*
  - – If he stole second and then was STRANDED (left on base when the inning ended), the entry in the scorecard for that player during the inning would be:

SCORECARD

NO.	POS	1	2	3	4	5	6	7	8	9	10	AB 11	R 12	H 13	RBI 14
	R														
	H														

BB = Bases on Balls	HBP = Hit by Pitch	S = Sacrifice Bunt	P = Popped Out
Bk = Balk	K or SO = Strikeout	SF = Sacrifice Fly	F = Flied Out
E = Error	PB = Passed Ball	WP = Wild Pitch	1B = Single
FC = Fielder's Choice	SB = Stolen Base	L = Lined Out	2B = Double

3B = Triple	Interference	7 = Left Fielder
HR = Home Run	CS = Caught Stealing	8 = Center Fielder
U = Unassisted	1 = Pitcher	9 = Right Fielder
CI = Catcher's	2 = Catcher	
	3 = 1st Baseman	
	4 = 2nd Baseman	
	5 = 3rd Baseman	
	6 = Shortstop	

– If he hit a triple and then scored on a ground out by the next hitter, the scorecard entry would be:

The diamond is shaded in so that runs stand out when they are counted up.

In each box of the scorecard, show how a player made an out (if he did not reach base safely).

- ◆ This is done by recording the number(s) of the defensive players who were given credit for the assist and for the putout. For example, if the batter hit a ground ball to the shortstop (6) who threw the ball to first base (3), this action would be recorded as follows:

6 – 3

- ◆ If the batter made an out by striking out, just write a K, (or a backward K if it was a called third strike):

K

- ◆ If a batted ball is caught by a fielder, include an L, F or P before the fielder's number to indicate a line out, pop out or fly out. For example, if the batter lined out to the left fielder, note it as follows:

L 7

When a substitution is made, write the new player's name underneath the replaced player. Next to the new player's name, put the inning number in which he first bats in parentheses. This helps to distinguish the substitute player's offensive performance from the original player's.

BOX SCORE

PIRATES 3, CUBS 0

Pittsburgh	ab	r	h	bi	bb	so	avg
Colby rf	3	0	0	0	0	1	.282
b-Estes ph-cf	1	0	0	0	0	0	.263
Benjamin ss	3	1	1	0	0	0	.268
Garson ss	0	0	0	1	0	0	.211
Vansing cf	4	1	2	2	0	1	.326
Coolidge p	0	0	0	0	0	0	.333
Bolling lf	4	0	0	0	0	0	.313
Benson p	0	0	0	0	0	0	.667
Kimber 3b	3	0	0	0	0	0	.235
Wellman 3b-2b	1	0	0	0	0	0	.179
Mercury 1b	4	0	1	0	0	1	.250
Lawson c	3	0	0	0	0	0	.257
Preston c	1	0	0	0	0	0	.100
Lipson 2b	3	0	1	0	0	0	.236
1-Young pr-3b	0	0	0	0	0	0	.571
Smithson p	1	0	0	0	0	0	.122
Watson p	1	0	1	0	0	0	.333
a-Vargo ph-rf	1	1	1	0	0	0	.222
Totals	**33**	**3**	**7**	**3**	**0**	**3**	

Chicago	ab	r	h	bi	bb	so	avg
Daley cf	3	0	0	0	1	0	.255
Argo ss	3	0	0	0	0	0	.298
c-Grant ph	1	0	0	0	0	0	.306
Sanders 2b	4	0	1	0	0	0	.298
Dawner rf	3	0	0	0	0	0	.278
Salvatore 3b	3	0	1	0	0	0	.204
Astor p	0	0	0	0	0	0	.000
Scranton p	0	0	0	0	0	0	.000
Villery 1b	3	0	0	0	0	2	.152
Wilson c	3	0	0	0	0	0	.267
Ramsey cf	3	0	0	0	0	0	.125
Casten p	2	0	0	0	0	0	.097
Bunson 3b	1	0	0	0	0	0	.260
Totals	**29**	**0**	**2**	**0**	**1**	**2**	

Pittsburgh			000 200 010—	3 7 1
Chicago			000 000 000—	0 2 0

a-singled for Watson in the 8th. b-grounded into fielder's choice for Colby in the 8th. c-safe on error for Argo in the 9th. 1-ran for Lipson in the 8th. Errors: Young (1). Left on base: Pittsburgh 4, Chicago 3. Doubles: Mercury (28). Home runs: Vansing (14) off Casten. Runs batted in: Garson (4), Vansing 2 (88). Sacrifice flies: Garson. Grounded into double play: Villery. Runners left in scoring position: Pittsburgh 1 (Preston) Chicago 0. Runners moved up: Estes. Double plays: Pittsburgh 1 (Benjamin, Lipson and Mercury).

PITCHERS

Pittsburgh	ip	h	r	er	bb	so	np	era
Smithson	3	1	0	0	0	0	35	3.11
Watson (W, 2-0)	4	1	0	0	1	1	52	0.69
Coolidge	1	0	0	0	0	1	9	3.74
Benson (S, 18)	1	0	0	0	0	0	14	3.18

Chicago	ip	h	r	er	bb	so	np	era
Casten (L, 9-11)	7	6	3	3	0	2	100	3.56
Astor	1⅓	0	0	0	0	1	15	4.05
Scranton	⅔	1	0	0	0	0	6	2.89

Casten pitched to 2 batters in the 8th. Inherited runners, number scored: Astor 2-1. Umpires: Home, Pullman; First, Hanson; Second, McShane; Third, Davis; Time: 2:14. Attend: 18, 759.

BOX SCORE — A complete summary of the game's action, based on compiling all of the entries from the scorecard. It appears in the sports page of the newspaper in addition to the narrative highlights of the game.

♦ Common *hitting* terms and their abbreviations in a box score include:

– Official At Bats (ab) — The number of times a player batted during the game minus the total number of times he was hit by a pitch, walked, reached base on a catcher's interference, had a sacrifice bunt or hit a sacrifice fly. For example, if a player struck out three times, hit one sacrifice fly and walked once, he would have three official at bats, since the sacrifice fly and walk do not count.

– Runs Scored (r) — The number of times a player reached home plate safely.

– Hits (h) — the number of base hits by a player.

– Runs Batted In (bi or rbi) — Credit given to a batter when a run scores as a result of his base hit, sacrifice bunt (either safety or suicide squeeze), sacrifice fly, ground out, bases-loaded walk or being hit by a pitch with the bases loaded.

  1. No rbi is awarded when a batter hits into a double play (with no outs), while a runner on third scores.

  2. No rbi is awarded to the batter when an error allows a runner to score.

  3. An rbi is awarded to a batter who hits a home run. He earns one for scoring himself, in addition to the rbi's he receives for any teammates who were on base.

– Base on balls (bb) — The number of times a batter walked during the game.

– Strikeout (so) — The number of times a batter struck out during the game.

Ted Williams, known as the "Splendid Splinter," was the last player to have a batting average of .400 or better. Williams batted .406 in 1941, which means over 40% of his official at bats resulted in base hits. In 1980, George Brett had a .400 batting average with two weeks left in the season, but faded to a season-ending .390.

– Batting Average (avg) — The primary way to measure a hitter's success. It is calculated by the following ratio:

$$\frac{\text{Total base hits}}{\text{Total official at bats}}$$

(e.g. $100 \div 300 = .333$)

1. A batting average is usually expressed in decimal form carried out to 3 places.

   a. If a player has 100 hits in 300 at bats, he has a .333 batting average (100/300). This player's batting average shows that 33% of his official at bats have resulted in a base hit.

   b. When reciting a player's batting average, the decimal place is ignored. In the above example, it is said that the player has a "333" batting average.

2. A batting average greater than .300 is considered excellent.

3. A batting average less than .250 is poor.

– Left on Base (LOB) — The number of base runners who were "stranded" at the inning's conclusion.

1. If the bases are loaded with two out, and a batter hits a grounder to the shortstop who then throws to the second baseman for the third out (fielder's choice), three men are considered to have been left on base (the runners who were originally on second and third base plus the batter).

2. If a team has left a lot of men on base during a game (10 or more), it is apparent that there were many wasted scoring opportunities.

*Famous baseball announcer
Milo Hamilton once made the
following suggestion when an Atlanta
Braves losing pitcher gave up a lot
of unearned runs during a game
because of his teammates' errors:
"He should take his fellow Braves
to divorce court on grounds
of non-support."*

◆ Common *pitching* terms and their abbreviations in a box score include:

– Innings Pitched (ip) — the number of innings pitched during the game by a pitcher. Each out counts as one third of an inning.

   1. If a starting pitcher is taken out of the game by his manager after two outs in the seventh inning, he is credited with pitching 6⅔ innings (6 full innings plus 2 of 3 outs in the seventh inning).

   2. If a starting pitcher faces one or more batters in the eighth inning without an out and is then replaced by a relief pitcher, he is credited with pitching only 7 innings.

– Hits (h) — The number of base hits a pitcher gave up in a game.

– Runs (r) — The number of batters a pitcher faced who eventually scored.

   1. A pitcher walks the leadoff hitter in an inning and is then replaced by a relief pitcher who gives up a home run to the next batter. Two runs score.

      a. The first pitcher is held accountable for one run because the batter he walked eventually scored during the inning.

      b. The other run is charged to the relief pitcher, since the batter hit the home run off of his pitch.

– Earned Runs (er) — The number of batters a pitcher faced who eventually scored without the benefit of errors or a catcher's passed ball. Runs that score due to errors or a catcher's passed ball are called UNEARNED RUNS.

   1. A leadoff batter hits a ground ball that the shortstop does not field cleanly, causing an error. The next batter hits a triple, scoring the run. The run is *unearned* because it scored due to the shortstop's error.

In 1973, 18-year-old David Clyde pitched for his Houston Westchester High School baseball team. Clyde had unbelievable statistics during his senior year including a microscopic 0.18 ERA. This means for every 50 innings Clyde pitched that year, he only gave up one earned run! (He also had an 18-0 won-loss record, striking out 328 hitters in 148 innings—more than two per inning). On June 27, 1973, less than three weeks after his high-school graduation, Clyde pitched for the Texas Rangers in the American League earning the win in a 4-3 victory over the Minnesota Twins. Unfortunately his major league career went downhill. When he retired 6 years later, his major league lifetime ERA was 4.63, winning 18 and losing 33.

2. If there are two outs in the inning, and a batter reaches base safely due to an error, all runs that score before the third out happens are unearned, because the inning should have already been over.

3. A pitcher who gives up a lot of unearned runs can partially blame his teammates for their poor fielding.

– Bases on Balls (bb) — The number of walks a pitcher gave up during the game.

– Strikeouts (so) — The number of times a pitcher got batters out on strikes during the game.

– Number of Pitches (np) — The total number of times a pitcher threw to batters during the game.

– Earned Run Average (era) — An important way to measure a pitcher's success. It is computed for each pitcher by using the following ratio:

$$\frac{\text{Total earned runs}}{\text{Total innings pitched}} \times 9$$

1. If a pitcher pitched 90 total innings and gave up 25 earned runs, his ERA is 2.50 (25/90 x 9). For every nine innings he has pitched, he has allowed 2½ earned runs.

2. When reciting the earned run average in the above example, it is said that the pitcher has a "2 point 5 oh" ERA.

a. An ERA less than 3.50 is excellent.

b. An ERA greater than 4.50 is poor.

– Winning Pitcher (W) — Another important way to measure a pitcher's success.

1. A *starting pitcher* gets the win if he pitches five innings or more, his team is winning before a relief pitcher enters the game and his team retains the lead for the remainder of the game.

Mike Marshall, a relief pitcher on the 1974 Los Angeles Dodgers, definitely deserved a rest when that season was completed. He set a record that still stands, by pitching in 106 games during that year or 65% of the Dodgers' games. His durabiliy earned him the nickname, "Iron Mike."

2. A *relief pitcher* gets the win if his team takes the lead after he has pitched at least 1/3 of an inning. The team must be in the lead before another relief pitcher enters the game, and the team must retain the lead for the remainder of the game.

  a. Say the Braves are tied with the Cardinals 3-3. A Braves relief pitcher pitches all three outs of the bottom of the eighth inning for the Braves and gives up no runs. In the top of the ninth, a pinch hitter for the relief pitcher hits a home run for a 4-3 lead. A second relief pitcher pitches for the Braves in the bottom of the ninth inning without giving up a run. The Braves win, and the first relief pitcher is the winning pitcher since he pitched at least ⅓ of an inning and the Braves took the lead (which they never relinquished) before another relief pitcher came into the game.

BRAVES	020	100	001
CARDINALS	300	000	000

  b. If the second relief pitcher had given up a run during the three outs he pitched in the ninth inning, but the Braves scored another run in the tenth inning to win the game, the first relief pitcher would not be the winning pitcher. The reason is the Braves did not retain the lead for the rest of the game (after he was removed). It was later tied 4-4 after he left, so the second relief pitcher is the winning pitcher.

BRAVES	020	100	001	1
CARDINALS	300	000	001	0

3. A pitcher is considered to be "among the elite" if he has 20 wins in a season.

*Not all pitchers are poor hitters.
On July 3, 1966, Atlanta Braves
pitcher Tony Cloninger hit two grand
slams in the same game. That's right,
two home runs with the bases loaded
were hit by a pitcher. Cloninger also
had a single that scored another run,
giving him 9 RBIs for the game.
That is a month's work for
many everyday players.*

– Losing Pitcher (L) — The pitcher who gave up the run that put the opposing team in the lead for the rest of the game. The number of innings pitched is not a determining factor of who is the losing pitcher. A starting pitcher who pitched less than five innings can be the losing pitcher.

    1. Assume the Braves' starting pitcher walks the Mets' leadoff hitter in the first inning and then has to leave the game with a pulled muscle. A relief pitcher replaces him and gives up a home run to the next hitter. He gives up no more runs for the rest of the game, but the Braves only scored one run in the seventh inning to lose 2-1. Who is the Braves' losing pitcher for the game?

| METS | 200 | 000 | 000 |
| BRAVES | 000 | 000 | 100 |

    2. The starting pitcher is the loser, because he faced a batter who eventually scored in that inning and gave the opposition a lead they never relinquished (even though he had only faced the one batter).

– Save (S) — A way to measure the success of a relief pitcher.

    1. A save is awarded to the winning team's *game-ending* relief pitcher, who entered the game with the *potential tying* run on base, at bat, or scheduled to hit next (called being ON DECK).

      a. A relief pitcher comes into the game in the ninth inning with his team leading 5-0. The bases are loaded with 2 outs, and the batter hits the ball over the fence for a GRAND SLAM (a home run with the bases loaded) to make it 5-4. The next hitter (the potential tying run on deck) hit a fly ball out to the center fielder. The relief pitcher would get the save.

Rickey Henderson ran through 1982 when he stole 130 bases during that year to set a modern-day (post-1900) single-season record. But he also set a single-season record for getting caught stealing 42 times during that same year.

2. A pitcher can also earn a save if he enters the game with a three-run lead, pitches at least one inning and finishes the game without giving up his team's lead for the rest of the game.

3. A save can be earned if the game-ending pitcher on the winning team pitches three innings regardless of the score, and is "effective" (subjectively determined by the official scorekeeper).

◆ The box score indicates which players were credited with the following statistics during the game: errors, doubles, triples, home runs, runs batted in, stolen bases and CAUGHT STEALING (tagged out while attempting to steal a base). Next to the player's name, in parentheses, is his season total for that statistic. Other statistics are listed, such as who had a sacrifice bunt or a sacrifice fly, but the season totals are not shown.

    – Pitchers' season totals for wins and losses are displayed next to both the winning and losing pitchers.

    – A pitcher's season total for saves is listed next to the relief pitcher, if any, who earned a save during the game.

*In some stadiums, such as
the Chicago Cubs' Wrigley Field, the
outfield seats are called BLEACHERS.
This term comes from the fact that
the sun caused these seats to change
color and have a "bleached" look.*

LEAGUE STRUCTURE AND TEAM STANDINGS

The STANDINGS show the position of each team within its division based on its wins and losses.

There are two leagues, with three divisions in each league:

NATIONAL LEAGUE

East Division
Atlanta Braves
Florida Marlins
Montreal Expos
New York Mets
Philadelphia Phillies

Central Division
Chicago Cubs
Cincinnati Reds
Houston Astros
Pittsburgh Pirates
St. Louis Cardinals

West Division
Colorado Rockies
Los Angeles Dodgers
San Diego Padres
San Francisco Giants

AMERICAN LEAGUE

East Division
Baltimore Orioles
Boston Red Sox
Detroit Tigers
New York Yankees
Toronto Blue Jays

Central Division
Chicago White Sox
Cleveland Indians
Kansas City Royals
Milwaukee Brewers
Minnesota Twins

West Division
California Angels
Oakland Athletics
Seattle Mariners
Texas Rangers

During the last few weeks of each season, baseball fans frequently use the term, MAGIC NUMBER, in addition to GAMES BACK to describe how far a team is from first place. The magic number is the combination of wins by the first-place team and losses by the second-place team that makes it impossible for the second-place team finish in first place before the season ends.

To compute the magic number, subtract both the first-place team's total wins and the second-place team's total losses from 163. For example, assume the first-place and second-place teams in the National League West Division had the following records:

	W	L
Los Angeles	90	63
San Francisco	87	67

The magic number would be 6, (163 less 90 less 67.) So if Los Angeles wins 4 more games, San Francisco must lose at least 2 more (to equal the magic number of 6) for Los Angeles to be division champs.

Common abbreviations and terms used in the team standings:

- ◆ W (wins) — The total wins by a team during the season.

- ◆ L (losses) — The total losses by a team during the season.

- ◆ Pct. (winning percentage) — The ratio of a team's total wins to total games played.

  - The winning percentage is recited as a 3-digit decimal. A team that has won 15 games and lost 5 has a .750 Pct. (15/20).

  - A team that has won and lost the same amount of games has a .500 Pct. and is commonly referred to as "at 500." For teams that do not usually win a lot of games, being "at 500" is a significant accomplishment.

- ◆ GB (games back) — The number of games a team needs to win (while the first-place team loses the same number) in order to tie for first place.

  - A team gains "a half game" on the first-place team when: that team either wins a game, or the first-place team loses a game. If the team defeats the first-place team in its division, it gains "two half games" or a *full* game in the standings.

  - A team loses a half game on the first-place team when: that team either loses a game, or the first place team wins a game. If the team loses a game, while the first-place team in its division wins its game, then the team drops two half games or one full game in the standings.

NATIONAL LEAGUE

EAST	W	L	Pct.	GB	L10	Streak	Home	Night	Grass	vs.RHP
New York	104	58	.642	—	7-3	Lost 1	51-30	77-43	82-43	75-43
Montreal	94	68	.580	10	7-3	Won 1	55-26	73-40	25-24	66-47
Florida	84	78	.519	20	6-4	Won 1	43-38	43-32	66-58	68-52
Philadelphia	73	89	.451	31	4-6	Won 2	41-40	50-63	19-30	56-62
Atlanta	61	101	.377	43	2-8	Lost 3	34-47	41-71	50-76	41-69
CENTRAL	**W**	**L**	**Pct.**	**GB**	**L10**	**Streak**	**Home**	**Night**	**Grass**	**vs.RHP**
Chicago	97	65	.599	—	4-6	Lost 2	52-29	72-45	30-19	63-47
Houston	87	75	.537	10	5-5	Won 2	49-32	56-56	27-22	61-58
Pittsburgh	81	81	.500	16	3-7	Won 1	41-40	60-57	64-61	61-56
Cincinnati	67	95	.414	30	4-6	Lost 4	39-42	42-62	53-71	54-75
St. Louis	64	98	.395	33	2-8	Lost 6	35-46	49-78	54-70	43-74
WEST	**W**	**L**	**Pct.**	**GB**	**L10**	**Streak**	**Home**	**Night**	**Grass**	**vs.RHP**
Los Angeles	103	59	.636	—	8-2	Lost 1	50-31	49-33	78-46	72-35
San Francisco	85	77	.525	18	6-4	Lost 2	44-37	56-54	27-24	57-51
San Diego	75	87	.463	28	5-5	Won 1	40-42	55-63	26-27	56-57
Colorado	59	103	.364	44	7-3	Won 6	28-53	38-64	47-77	49-70

Tug McGraw, a former pitcher with the New York Mets and Philadelphia Phillies, was once asked which he prefered, grass or artificial turf? He replied, "I don't know, I've never smoked artificial turf."

- L10 (Last 10) — Displays the won-loss record of a team's previous 10 games. If a team's entry in this column is 8-2, that means it has won 8 and lost 2 in its previous ten games.

- Streak — Indicates the result of each team's most recent game and how many consecutive previous games had the same result.

  - If the standings show "Won 6," it means the team has won 6 games in a row.

  - If the standings show "Lost 1," it means the team lost its last game.

- Home — Shows how many games a team has won and lost on its own playing field. To determine the team's "road" record, just subtract the home losses from the total losses and the home wins from the total wins.

- Night — Shows how many games a team has won and lost at night. To determine the team's "day" record, just subtract the night losses from the total losses and the night wins from the total wins.

- Grass — Shows how many games a team has won and lost while playing on a natural field (with grass). To determine the team's "artificial surface" record, just subtract the "grass" losses from the total losses and the "grass" wins from the total wins.

- vs. RHP (Versus Right-Handed Pitchers) — Shows a team's performance in games where the opposing team's pitcher (who was credited with the win or loss) was right-handed. To determine the team's record against left-handed pitchers, subtract the "right-handed" losses from the total losses and the "right-handed" wins from the total wins.

From 1943 to 1945, teams conducted spring training in the northeastern part of the country to avoid long train trips. This was to minimize the use of such valued transportation during the war effort. Many teams had to practice inside gyms because of the cold weather.

BASEBALL SEASON CYCLE

Spring Training — The 6-to-8-week period from the end of February to the beginning of April, when teams get into shape and prepare for the regular season.

- Most teams train in Florida cities, but a few train in Arizona and Southern California.
- The teams practice among themselves and also play exhibition games against other teams.
- Spring training helps the manager decide who will be on the 25-man team (ROSTER) for the beginning of the regular season. (On September 1st of each season, a team may expand its roster to 40 players.)

Regular Season — The 6-month, 162-game schedule of games each team plays.

- The primary objective of each team is to finish in first place in its division, and therefore advance to the playoffs. Teams from one league do not play teams from the other league during the regular season.
- The second-place team with the best percentage in each league also qualifies for the playoffs and is called the WILD CARD team.

First Round Of Playoffs — In each league, the division winner with the best record plays the wild card team, while the other two division winners play each other. The games take place during the beginning of October.

- If the team with the best record and the wild card team are from the same division, they do not play each other in the first round of the playoffs. Instead, the division winner with the second-best record plays the wild card team, while the remaining two division winners play each other.

A famous World Series moment took place in Game 3 of the 1932 Fall Classic between the New York Yankees and the Chicago Cubs. The Chicago fans and players were trying to unnerve the Yankee star right fielder, Babe Ruth, by (among other things) throwing lemons at him. After he had an 0 and 2 count in the fifth inning, he pointed toward the flagpole beyond the center field fence, which is exactly where the next pitch landed for a home run. Babe laughed uncontrollably as he rounded the bases.

◆ The teams play each other in a series of games that continue until one team wins three games.

    – The maximum possible number of games in the first round series is five, with one team winning three games and the other team winning two.

    – Therefore, the length of the first round of the playoffs is said to be the BEST 3 OUT OF 5.

    – The minimum number of games that could be played in a best 3 out of 5 series is three, with one team winning the first three games, ending the series.

League Championship Playoffs — The two first-round play-off winners in each league play each other in a best 4 out of 7 series. The winners are called the National League Champions and the American League Champions.

The World Series — The National League Champions and the American League Champions play each other in another best 4 out of 7 series. Sometimes it is referred to as the FALL CLASSIC. The winning team earns the title of World Champion.

INDEX

BASEBALL QUIZ #1

1. If the teams are tied after nine innings. *What happens?*
   a. The game results in a tie.
   b. The team that scores the next run automatically wins, and the game ends at that time.
   c. The teams continue playing, and the game ends when one team scores more runs than the other in an inning.
   d. The teams play another nine innings.

2. If a batted ball bounces off third base. *What happens?*
   a. It is a fair ball.
   b. It is a foul ball.
   c. It is a dead ball, and play automatically stops.
   d. Third base interference is called.

3. There are runners on first base and second base. A ball is hit to the left fielder who catches it after it bounces once. He then throws the ball all the way to the catcher who merely holds on to it while touching home plate. The runner originally on second base arrives at home plate a split second later. *What happens?*
   a. That runner is out.
   b. That runner is safe and therefore a run is scored.
   c. That runner must go back to third base.
   d. That runner bats next.

4. The leadoff batter in the inning strikes out, but on the last strike the catcher drops the ball. *What happens?*
   a. The batter is automatically out.
   b. The batter is automatically safe.
   c. The batter is safe if he arrives at first base before an opposing player touches that base with the ball in his possession.
   d. The inning is over.

5. The leadoff hitter in the inning walks, and the second batter strikes out with the catcher dropping the ball on the third strike. *What happens?*

   a. The batter is automatically out.
   b. The batter is automatically safe.
   c. The batter is safe if he arrives at first base before an opposing player touches that base with the ball in his possession.
   d. The inning is over.

6. The first two batters in the inning make outs. The third hitter goes to first base, because he was hit by a pitch. The next hitter strikes out, but the catcher drops the ball on the third strike. *What happens?*

   a. The batter is automatically out.
   b. The batter is automatically safe.
   c. The batter is safe if he arrives at first base before an opposing player touches that base with the ball in his possession.
   d. The runner on first base is out if he arrives at second base after an opposing player touches that base with the ball in his possession.
   e. "c." and "d."

7. What kind of pitch is generally the most difficult for catchers to catch?

   a. Fastball.
   b. Curveball.
   c. Knuckle ball.
   d. Slider.

8. If a ground ball is hit to the first baseman's right side drawing him off the base and he misses it but the second baseman fields it, whose responsibility is it to cover first base?

   a. Pitcher.
   b. Catcher.
   c. First baseman.
   d. Right fielder.

BASEBALL QUIZ #1 (CONT'D)

9. If there is a runner on first base and the pitcher throws the next pitch over the batter's head enabling the runner to advance to second base, which term describes what happened?

   a. Wild pitch.
   b. Passed ball.
   c. Error.
   d. Caught stealing.

10. The best defensive infielder most likely plays what position?

   a. Third base.
   b. Second base.
   c. First base.
   d. Shortstop.

ANSWERS TO BASEBALL QUIZ #1

1. (c) The game goes into extra innings.

2. (a) First and third base are placed on the field in such a way that the entire base is in fair territory (including the edge of the base lined up with the foul line). If a base is hit by a batted ball, it is a fair ball.

3. (b) The runner is safe, because he was not forced to go to home plate. (He was forced to go to third base, not home.) Therefore, the catcher must tag the runner for the out.

4. (c) The only time a batter is automatically out on a catcher's dropped third strike is if first base is occupied, and there are less than two outs. Because he was the leadoff batter in this case, first base could not have been occupied.

5. (a) First base was occupied with less than two outs, so a catcher's dropped third strike is an automatic out.

6. (e) Both the runner and the batter are forced to go to the next base when the catcher drops the third strike and there are two outs. (Remember that the batter is not automatically out because there were two outs.) Since the force out rules are applicable, both "c" and "d" are correct.

7. (c) The knuckle ball is thrown in such a manner that the ball does not have its natural spin, causing it to move unpredictably toward home plate and making it difficult to catch.

8. (a) The pitcher should always run to cover first base any time the ball is hit to the right side of the infield.

9. (a) When a catcher misses a pitched ball allowing a runner to advance a base and it is the pitcher's fault, it is called a wild pitch. If it were the catcher's fault, it would be a passed ball.

10. (d) Because a shortstop has a wide area to cover (including the part of that area to his right that is farthest from first base), he usually has the most fielding talent and a strong throwing arm.

BASEBALL QUIZ #2

Pretend you are the team's manager in the following situations:

1. Your team is batting in the ninth inning and losing by three runs. *What would you have your first hitter in the inning do if the count is 3 and 0?*
   - a. Swing and try to hit a home run.
   - b. Take the pitch in hope of a walk.
   - c. Bunt the ball to try to get to first base.
   - d. Steal second base.

2. Your left-handed-hitting platooned right fielder is scheduled to hit first in the eighth inning, and you are down by one run. The opposing manager inserts a left-handed relief pitcher. *What would you do?*
   - a. Pinch hit with a right-handed batter.
   - b. Let the scheduled left-handed hitter bat.
   - c. Pinch hit with a left-handed batter.
   - d. Instruct him to sacrifice bunt.

3. Your leadoff hitter in the first inning hit a double. *What would you do with your second hitter?*
   - a. Sacrifice bunt.
   - b. Pinch hit for him.
   - c. Instruct him to hit it to the right side.
   - d. "a" or "c"

4. In the fifth inning of a scoreless game your eighth hitter in the lineup hit a single with one out. *What would you do if your pitcher was scheduled to bat next?*
   - a. Pinch hit for the pitcher.
   - b. Instruct the pitcher to sacrifice bunt.
   - c. Instruct the pitcher to hit it to the right side.
   - d. Instruct the pitcher to hit a pop fly in the infield.

5. Your team is losing by one run in the bottom of the ninth inning. Your first two batters in the inning walked. Your leadoff hitter in the batting order is scheduled to hit. *What would you do?*
   - a. Put on the hit and run play.
   - b. Instruct him to hit to the right side.
   - c. Instruct him to sacrifice bunt.
   - d. Instruct him to take the pitch when the count is 0 and 2.

BASEBALL QUIZ #2 (CONT'D)

6. The opposing team was successful in the same situation as in question 5, so that there are now runners on second and third with one out. Their number two hitter, who is left-handed, is scheduled to face your best right-handed relief pitcher. The following hitter is right-handed. *What would you do?*

      a. Intentionally walk the left-handed hitter.
      b. Bring in a substitute left-handed relief pitcher.
      c. Bring in a substitute catcher.
      d. Instruct the pitcher to throw a wild pitch.

7. Your team is losing by one run in the bottom of the seventh inning. Your right-handed starting pitcher looks tired, and there is an opposing runner on third base with two outs. You have one of your best relief pitchers ready in the bullpen. Next inning, the pitcher is scheduled to hit first for your team. *What do you do?*

      a. Intentionally walk the next hitter.
      b. Double switch. Bring in the relief pitcher and another substitute at the fielding position of the player who had batted first in the batting order. Bat the substitute fielder in the ninth spot in the batting order and the relief pitcher in the first spot.
      c. Double Switch. Bring in the relief pitcher and another substitute at the fielding position of the player who had batted eighth in the batting order. Bat the substitute fielder in the ninth spot in the batting order and the relief pitcher in the eighth spot.
      d. Instruct the pitcher to throw a pitchout.

8. You feel that the opposing runner on first base will be stealing on the next pitch. The count is one ball and two strikes with two out. *What do you do?*

      a. Instruct the pitcher to throw a pitch close to the batter (BRUSHBACK PITCH).
      b. Instruct the pitcher to throw a pitchout.
      c. Instruct the pitcher to take a full windup.
      d. Instruct the pitcher to balk.

BASEBALL QUIZ #2 (CONT'D)

9. The opposing team has runners on first, second and third base with no outs in the bottom of the ninth inning of a tie game. Your best left-handed relief pitcher is facing their best left-handed hitter. *What would you do?*

    a. Play the infield in.
    b. Bring in a right-handed relief pitcher.
    c. Order a pitchout when the count is 2 and 0.
    d. Intentionally walk the hitter.

10. The count on the opposing leadoff batter in the first inning is no balls and two strikes. *What would you like to see your pitcher do?*

    a. Waste a pitch.
    b. Intentionally walk the batter.
    c. Throw the pitch across the middle of home plate.
    d. Make a pickoff throw to first base.

ANSWERS TO BASEBALL QUIZ #2

1. (b) When a team is losing by more than one run in the ninth inning, its first priority is to put runners on base, so they can eventually score (called a RALLY).

2. (a) The reason a player is platooned is because he does not hit as well when facing a pitcher who throws from the same side as he bats (remember the "BOPS" principle). Since your team is in dire need of a run late in the game, a right-handed pinch hitter is in order. (Most likely, you would use the right-handed-hitting platooned right fielder who would also enter the game defensively, saving you from having to use another player.)

3. (d) The idea is to advance the runner to third base with less than two outs, so he can score if a subsequent batter hits a sacrifice fly. A conservative manager would use the safer solution by calling for a sacrifice bunt. A more aggressive manager would call for his batter to hit the ball on the ground to the right side of the infield, which might go through to the outfield for a base hit.

4. (b) You want to accomplish two things. First, advance the runner to second base (scoring position) so that a subsequent hitter could score him with a single or another type of base hit and break the scoreless tie. Second, avoid the double play ground ball so that upcoming hitters will have a runner on base when it is their turn to bat. The sacrifice bunt accomplishes both.

5. (c) Here, you want to accomplish three similar objectives mentioned in the above two solutions. You want to advance runners into scoring position where a subsequent single should bring them both home to win the game. It is also important to advance a runner to third base with less than two outs so that he may score the tying run on a sacrifice fly. Finally, avoid the double play ground ball which would nearly kill the rally. The sacrifice bunt meets all three objectives.

6. (a) Once again, you have three objectives to accomplish. First, give the opposing team a chance to kill their rally by hitting a ground ball double play when there is a runner on first. Second, play the percentages by allowing your right-handed pitcher to throw to right-handed hitters. Third, keep your best relief pitcher in the game by not substituting for him. The intentional walk to the left-handed batter gives you all three.

7. (c) A double switch is the correct call. When this strategy is used during a pitching change, ordinarily the player who ended the previous inning is also replaced, and the new pitcher bats in his spot in the lineup. This means the new pitcher will be the ninth hitter scheduled to bat in later innings, avoiding the "pinch hitting" decision for a while. You will most likely have one of your best relief pitchers able to not only finish the seventh inning, but also the eighth and ninth, if necessary. Note that (b) is incorrect even though it is also a double switch. All (b) does is postpone the pitcher's time at bat by just one spot in the batting order.

8. (b) A pitchout gives your catcher an advantage in getting out of his crouched position early to receive the pitch and throw out the runner. Don't forget that you would not call for a pitchout when the count is two or three balls.

9. (a) An infielder who fields a ground ball at his normal position is far enough from home plate that a runner on third would usually score before his throw reaches home plate. Remember that the runner on third already has a head start toward home plate because of his lead off the base.

10. (a) Tempt the opposing batter by throwing a pitch outside of the strike zone which would be difficult to hit. If the batter does not swing, your pitcher will still be ahead in the count: 1 ball, 2 strikes.

BIBLIOGRAPHY

Benagh, Jim. *BASEBALL Startling Stories Behind the Records.*
Sterling Publishing, 1987.

Fusselle, Warner. *Baseball…A Laughing Matter.*
The Sporting News Publishing Co., 1987.

Gibson, Charlene. *A Wife's Guide to Baseball.*
The Viking Press, 1970.

Nash, Bruce. *The Baseball Hall of Fame.*
Pocket Books, 1985.

Nemec, David. *Great Baseball Feats, Facts and Firsts.*
New American Library, 1987.

Okrent, Daniel. *Baseball Anecdotes.*
Oxford University Press, 1989.

Reichler, Joseph. *The Great All-Time Baseball Record Book.*
MacMillan Publishing Co., 1993.

Schlossberg, Dan. *The Baseball Book of Why.*
Jonathan David Publishers, 1984.

Siwoff, Seymour. *Book of Baseball Records.*
Seymour Siwoff Publishing, 1993.

Spalding, Albert G. *America's National Game.*
Halo Books, 1991.

Sports Illustrated *1994 Sports Almanac.*
Little, Brown & Company (Canada) Limited, 1994.

Sudyk, Bob. *Me and the Spitter.*
Saturday Night Press, 1974.

Sugar, Bert Randolph. *Baseball Trivia Book to End All Baseball Trivia Books.*
Freundlich Books, 1986.

Thorn, John. *A Century of Baseball Lore.*
Hart Publishing, 1976.

Wagonner, Glen. *Baseball by the Rules.*
Taylor Publishing, 1987.

APPENDICES

MAJOR LEAGUE BASEBALL TICKET INFORMATION
LEAGUE OFFICE & TEAMS—ADDRESSES & PHONE NUMBERS

MAJOR LEAGUE BASEBALL 350 PARK AVENUE NEW YORK, NY 10022	212-339-7800
NATIONAL LEAGUE 350 PARK AVENUE NEW YORK, NY 10022	212-339-7700
ATLANTA BRAVES PO BOX 4064 ATLANTA, GA 30302	404-522-7630
CHICAGO CUBS 1061 WEST ADDISON STREET CHICAGO, IL 60613	312-404-2827
CINCINNATI REDS 100 RIVERFRONT STADIUM CINCINNATI, OH 45202	513-421-4510
COLORADO ROCKIES 1700 BROADWAY, SUITE 2100 DENVER, CO 80290	303-292-0200
FLORIDA MARLINS 2267 NW 199TH STREET MIAMI, FL 33056	305-626-7400
HOUSTON ASTROS PO BOX 288 HOUSTON, TX 77001	713-799-9500
LOS ANGELES DODGERS 1000 ELYSIAN PARK AVENUE LOS ANGELES, CA 90012	213-224-1500
MONTREAL EXPOS PO BOX 500, STATION M MONTREAL, QUEBEC H1V3P2	514-253-3434
NEW YORK METS SHEA STADIUM FLUSHING, NY 11368	718-507-6387
PHILADELPHIA PHILLIES PO BOX 7575 PHILADELPHIA, PA 19101	215-463-6000
PITTSBURGH PIRATES THREE RIVERS STADIUM PITTSBURGH, PA 15212	412-323-5000
ST. LOUIS CARDINALS 250 STADIUM PLAZA ST. LOUIS, MO 63102	314-421-3060
SAN DIEGO PADRES PO BOX 2000 SAN DIEGO, CA 92112	619-283-7294

SAN FRANCISCO GIANTS   415-468-3700
CANDLESTICK PARK
SAN FRANCISCO, CA 94124

AMERICAN LEAGUE   212-339-7600
350 PARK AVENUE
NEW YORK, NY 10022

BALTIMORE ORIOLES   410-685-9800
333 W. CAMDEN ST.
BALTIMORE, MD 21201

BOSTON RED SOX   617-267-9440
FENWAY PARK
BOSTON, MA 02215

CALIFORNIA ANGELS   714-937-7200
PO BOX 2000
ANAHEIM, CA 92803

CHICAGO WHITE SOX   312-924-1000
333 WEST 35TH STREET
CHICAGO, IL 60616

CLEVELAND INDIANS   216-420-4200
2401 ONTARIO STREET
CLEVELAND, OH 44115

DETROIT TIGERS   313-962-4000
2121 TRUMBULL AVENUE
DETROIT, MI 48216

KANSAS CITY ROYALS   816-921-2200
PO BOX 419969
KANSAS CITY, MO 64141

MILWAUKEE BREWERS   414-933-4114
COUNTY STADIUM
MILWAUKEE, WI 53214

MINNESOTA TWINS   612-375-1366
501 CHICAGO AVENUE SOUTH
MINNEAPOLIS, MN 55415

NEW YORK YANKEES   718-293-4300
YANKEE STADIUM
BRONX, NY 10451

OAKLAND ATHLETICS   510-638-4900
OAKLAND COLISEUM
OAKLAND, CA 94621

SEATTLE MARINERS   206-628-3555
PO BOX 4100
SEATTLE, WA 98104

TEXAS RANGERS   817-273-5222
PO BOX 90111
ARLINGTON, TX 76004

TORONTO BLUE JAYS   416-341-1000
THE SKYDOME
1 BLUE JAYS WAY #3200
TORONTO, ONTARIO M5V 1J1

1903	BOSTON (A) 5, PITTSBURGH (N) 3
1904	NO SERIES
1905	NEW YORK (N) 4, PHILADELPHIA (A) 1
1906	CHICAGO (A) 4, CHICAGO (N) 2
1907	CHICAGO (N) 4, DETROIT (A) 0; 1 TIE
1908	CHICAGO (N) 4, DETROIT (A) 1
1909	PITTSBURGH (N) 4, DETROIT (A) 3
1910	PHILADELPHIA (A) 4, CHICAGO (N) 1
1911	PHILADELPHIA (A) 4, NEW YORK (N) 2
1912	BOSTON (A) 4, NEW YORK (N) 3; 1 TIE
1913	PHILADELPHIA (A) 4, NEW YORK (N) 1
1914	BOSTON (N) 4, PHILADELPHIA (A) 0
1915	BOSTON (A) 4, PHILADELPHIA (N) 1
1916	BOSTON (A) 4, BROOKLYN (N) 1
1917	CHICAGO (A) 4, NEW YORK (N) 2
1918	BOSTON (A) 4, CHICAGO (N) 2
1919	CINCINNATI (N) 5, CHICAGO (A) 3
1920	CLEVELAND (A) 5, BROOKLYN (N) 2
1921	NEW YORK (N) 5, NEW YORK (A) 3
1922	NEW YORK (N) 4, NEW YORK (A) 0; 1 TIE
1923	NEW YORK (A) 4, NEW YORK (N) 2
1924	WASHINGTON (A) 4, NEW YORK (N) 3
1925	PITTSBURGH (N) 4, WASHINGTON (A) 3
1926	ST LOUIS (N) 4, NEW YORK (A) 3
1927	NEW YORK (A) 4, PITTSBURGH (N) 0
1928	NEW YORK (A) 4, ST LOUIS (N) 0
1929	PHILADELPHIA (A) 4, CHICAGO (N) 1
1930	PHILADELPHIA (A) 4, ST LOUIS (N) 2
1931	ST LOUIS (N) 4, PHILADELPHIA (A) 3
1932	NEW YORK (A) 4, CHICAGO (N) 0
1933	NEW YORK (N) 4, WASHINGTON (A) 1
1934	ST LOUIS (N) 4, DETROIT (A) 3
1935	DETROIT (A) 4, CHICAGO (N) 2
1936	NEW YORK (A) 4, NEW YORK (N) 2
1937	NEW YORK (A) 4, NEW YORK (N) 1
1938	NEW YORK (A) 4, CHICAGO (N) 0
1939	NEW YORK (A) 4, CINCINNATI (N) 0
1940	CINCINNATI (N) 4, DETROIT (A) 3
1941	NEW YORK (A) 4, BROOKLYN (N) 1
1942	ST LOUIS (N) 4, NEW YORK (A) 1
1943	NEW YORK (A) 4, ST LOUIS (N)1
1944	ST LOUIS (N) 4, ST LOUIS (A) 2
1945	DETROIT (A) 4, CHICAGO (N) 3
1946	ST LOUIS (N) 4, BOSTON (A) 3
1947	NEW YORK (A) 4, BROOKLYN (N) 3
1948	CLEVELAND (A) 4, BOSTON (N) 2
1949	NEW YORK (A) 4, BROOKLYN (N) 1
1950	NEW YORK (A) 4, PHILADELPHIA (N) 0
1951	NEW YORK (A) 4, NEW YORK (N) 2
1952	NEW YORK (A) 4, BROOKLYN (N) 3
1953	NEW YORK (A) 4, BROOKLYN (N) 2
1954	NEW YORK (N) 4, CLEVELAND (A) 0

1955	BROOKLYN (N) 4, NEW YORK (A) 3
1956	NEW YORK (A) 4, BROOKLYN (N) 3
1957	MILWAUKEE (N) 4, NEW YORK (A) 3
1958	NEW YORK (A) 4, MILWAUKEE (N) 3
1959	LOS ANGELES (N) 4, CHICAGO (A) 2
1960	PITTSBURGH (N) 4, NEW YORK (A) 3
1961	NEW YORK (A) 4, CINCINNATI (N) 1
1962	NEW YORK (A) 4, SAN FRANCISCO (N) 3
1963	LOS ANGELES (N) 4, NEW YORK (A) 0
1964	ST LOUIS (N) 4, NEW YORK (A) 3
1965	LOS ANGELES (N) 4, MINNESOTA (A) 3
1966	BALTIMORE (A) 4, LOS ANGELES (N) 0
1967	ST LOUIS (N) 4, BOSTON (A) 3
1968	DETROIT (A) 4, ST LOUIS (N) 3
1969	NEW YORK (N) 4, BALTIMORE (A) 1
1970	BALTIMORE (A) 4, CINCINNATI (N) 1
1971	PITTSBURGH (N) 4, BALTIMORE (A) 3
1972	OAKLAND (A) 4, CINCINNATI (N) 3
1973	OAKLAND (A) 4, NEW YORK (N) 3
1974	OAKLAND (A) 4, LOS ANGELES (N) 1
1975	CINCINNATI (N) 4, BOSTON (A) 3
1976	CINCINNATI (N) 4, NEW YORK (A) 0
1977	NEW YORK (A) 4, LOS ANGELES (N) 2
1978	NEW YORK (A) 4, LOS ANGELES (N) 2
1979	PITTSBURGH (N) 4, BALTIMORE (A) 3
1980	PHILADELPHIA (N) 4, KANSAS CITY (A) 2
1981	LOS ANGELES (N) 4, NEW YORK (A) 2
1982	ST LOUIS (N) 4, MILWAUKEE (A) 3
1983	BALTIMORE (A) 4, PHILADELPHIA (N) 1
1984	DETROIT (A) 4, SAN DIEGO (N) 1
1985	KANSAS CITY (A) 4, ST LOUIS (N) 3
1986	NEW YORK (N) 4, BOSTON (A) 3
1987	MINNESOTA (A) 4, ST LOUIS (N) 3
1988	LOS ANGELES (N) 4, OAKLAND (A) 1
1989	OAKLAND (A) 4, SAN FRANCISCO (N) 0
1990	CINCINNATI (N) 4, OAKLAND (A) 0
1991	MINNESOTA (A) 4, ATLANTA (N) 3
1992	TORONTO (A) 4, ATLANTA (N) 2
1993	TORONTO (A) 4, PHILADELPHIA (N) 2

WORLD SERIES MOST VALUABLE PLAYERS

1955	JOHNNY PODRES, BKLYN
1956	DON LARSEN, NY (A)
1957	LEW BURDETTE, MIL
1958	BOB TURLEY, NY (A)
1959	LARRY SHERRY, LA
1960	BOBBY RICHARDSON, NY (A)
1961	WHITEY FORD, NY (A)
1962	RALPH TERRY, NY (A)
1963	SANDY KOUFAX, LA
1964	BOB GIBSON, STL
1965	SANDY KOUFAX, LA
1966	FRANK ROBINSON, BALT

1967	BOB GIBSON, STL
1968	MICKEY LOLICH, DET
1969	DONN CLENDENON, NY (N)
1970	BROOKS ROBINSON, BALT
1971	ROBERTO CLEMENTE, PITT
1972	GENE TENACE, OAK
1973	REGGIE JACKSON, OAK
1974	ROLLIE FINGERS, OAK
1975	PETE ROSE, CIN
1976	JOHNNY BENCH, CIN
1977	REGGIE JACKSON, NY (A)
1978	BUCKY DENT, NY (A)
1979	WILLIE STARGELL, PITT
1980	MIKE SCHMIDT, PHIL
1981	RON CEY, LA
	PEDRO GUERRERO, LA
	STEVE YEAGER, LA
1982	DARRELL PORTER, STL
1983	RICK DEMPSEY, BALT
1984	ALAN TRAMMELL, DET
1985	BRET SABERHAGEN, KC
1986	RAY KNIGHT, NY (N)
1987	FRANK VIOLA, MINN
1988	OREL HERSHISER, LA
1989	DAVE STEWART, OAK
1990	JOSE RIJO, CIN
1991	JACK MORRIS, MINN
1992	PAT BORDERS, TOR
1993	PAUL MOLITOR, TOR

REGULAR SEASON CAREER BATTING LEADERS

GAMES

PETE ROSE	3562
CARL YASTRZEMSKI	3308
HANK AARON	3298
TY COBB	3034
STAN MUSIAL	3026
WILLIE MAYS	2992
RUSTY STAUB	2951
BROOKS ROBINSON	2896
ROBIN YOUNT	2856
DAVE WINFIELD	2850
AL KALINE	2834
EDDIE COLLINS	2826
REGGIE JACKSON	2820
FRANK ROBINSON	2808
TRIS SPEAKER	2789
HONUS WAGNER	2789
TONY PEREZ	2777

MEL OTT	2734
GEORGE BRETT	2707
GRAIG NETTLES	2700

AT BATS

PETE ROSE	14053
HANK AARON	12364
CARL YASTRZEMSKI	11988
TY COBB	11429
ROBIN YOUNT	11008
STAN MUSIAL	10972
WILLIE MAYS	10881
BROOKS ROBINSON	10654
DAVE WINFIELD	10594
HONUS WAGNER	10441
GEORGE BRETT	10349
LOU BROCK	10332
LUIS APARICIO	10230
TRIS SPEAKER	10208
AL KALINE	10116
RABBIT MARANVILLE	10078
FRANK ROBINSON	10006
EDDIE COLLINS	9949
REGGIE JACKSON	9864
TONY PEREZ	9778

HOME RUNS

HANK AARON	755
BABE RUTH	714
WILLIE MAYS	660
FRANK ROBINSON	586
HARMON KILLEBREW	573
REGGIE JACKSON	563
MIKE SCHMIDT	548
MICKEY MANTLE	536
JIMMIE FOXX	534
TED WILLIAMS	521
WILLIE MCCOVEY	521
EDDIE MATHEWS	512
ERNIE BANKS	512
MEL OTT	511
LOU GEHRIG	493
WILLIE STARGELL	475
STAN MUSIAL	475
DAVE WINFIELD	453
CARL YASTRZEMSKI	452
DAVE KINGMAN	442

HITS

PETE ROSE	4256
TY COBB	4191
HANK AARON	3771

```
STAN MUSIAL ...................................................................3630
TRIS SPEAKER ..................................................................3515
CARL YASTRZEMSKI..........................................................3419
HONUS WAGNER.............................................................3418
EDDIE COLLINS ................................................................3311
WILLIE MAYS....................................................................3283
NAP LAJOIE......................................................................3244
GEORGE BRETT ...............................................................3154
PAUL WANER ..................................................................3152
ROBIN YOUNT..................................................................3142
ROD CAREW ...................................................................3053
LOU BROCK.....................................................................3023
DAVE WINFIELD ..............................................................3014
AL KALINE.......................................................................3007
ROBERTO CLEMENTE .......................................................3000
CAP ANSON ....................................................................3000
SAM RICE ........................................................................2987
```

BATTING AVERAGE

```
TY COBB.......................................................................... .367
ROGERS HORNSBY............................................................ .358
JOE JACKSON .................................................................. .356
ED DELAHANTY................................................................ .346
TED WILLIAMS................................................................. .344
TRIS SPEAKER.................................................................. .344
BILLY HAMILTON .............................................................. .344
WILLIE KEELER.................................................................. .343
DAN BROUTHERS............................................................. .342
BABE RUTH ..................................................................... .342
HARRY HEILMANN ............................................................ .342
PETE BROWNING .............................................................. .341
BILL TERRY ...................................................................... .341
GEORGE SISLER ............................................................... .340
LOU GEHRIG.................................................................... .340
JESSE BURKETT................................................................. .339
NAP LAJOIE..................................................................... .338
RIGGS STEPHENSON ......................................................... .336
WADE BOGGS .................................................................. .335
AL SIMMONS.................................................................... .334
```

RUNS

```
TY COBB..........................................................................2245
BABE RUTH ......................................................................2174
HANK AARON...................................................................2174
PETE ROSE .......................................................................2165
WILLIE MAYS.....................................................................2062
STAN MUSIAL ...................................................................1949
LOU GEHRIG.....................................................................1888
TRIS SPEAKER ...................................................................1881
MEL OTT ..........................................................................1859
FRANK ROBINSON .............................................................1829
EDDIE COLLINS .................................................................1818
CARL YASTRZEMSKI.............................................................1816
```

TED WILLIAMS	1798
CHARLIE GEHRINGER	1774
JIMMIE FOXX	1751
HONUS WAGNER	1735
WILLIE KEELER	1727
CAP ANSON	1719
JESSE BURKETT	1718
BILLY HAMILTON	1692

DOUBLES

TRIS SPEAKER	792
PETE ROSE	746
STAN MUSIAL	725
TY COBB	724
GEORGE BRETT	665
NAP LAJOIE	658
CARL YASTRZEMSKI	646
HONUS WAGNER	643
HANK AARON	624
PAUL WANER	603
ROBIN YOUNT	583
CHARLIE GEHRINGER	574
HARRY HEILMANN	542
ROGERS HORNSBY	541
JOE MEDWICK	540
AL SIMMONS	539
LOU GEHRIG	535
AL OLIVER	529
CAP ANSON	528
FRANK ROBINSON	528

TRIPLES

SAM CRAWFORD	312
TY COBB	297
HONUS WAGNER	252
JAKE BECKLEY	243
ROGER CONNOR	233
TRIS SPEAKER	223
FRED CLARKE	220
DAN BROUTHERS	205
JOE KELLEY	194
PAUL WANER	190
BID MCPHEE	188
EDDIE COLLINS	187
SAM RICE	184
ED DELEHANTY	183
JESSE BURKETT	183
EDD ROUSH	182
ED KONETCHY	181
BUCK EWING	178
RABBIT MARANVILLE	177
STAN MUSIAL	177
HARRY STOVEY	177

BASES ON BALLS

BABE RUTH	2056
TED WILLIAMS	2019
JOE MORGAN	1865
CARL YASTRZEMSKI	1845
MICKEY MANTLE	1734
MEL OTT	1708
EDDIE YOST	1614
DARRELL EVANS	1605
STAN MUSIAL	1599
PETE ROSE	1566
HARMON KILLEBREW	1559
LOU GEHRIG	1508
MIKE SCHMIDT	1507
EDDIE COLLINS	1503
WILLIE MAYS	1463
JIMMIE FOXX	1452
EDDIE MATHEWS	1444
FRANK ROBINSON	1420
RICKEY HENDERSON	1406
HANK AARON	1402

RUNS BATTED IN

HANK AARON	2297
BABE RUTH	2211
LOU GEHRIG	1990
TY COBB	1961
STAN MUSIAL	1951
JIMMIE FOXX	1921
WILLIE MAYS	1903
MEL OTT	1861
CARL YASTRZEMSKI	1844
TED WILLIAMS	1839
AL SIMMONS	1827
FRANK ROBINSON	1812
DAVE WINFIELD	1786
HONUS WAGNER	1732
CAL ANSON	1715
REGGIE JACKSON	1702
EDDIE MURRAY	1662
TONY PEREZ	1652
ERNIE BANKS	1636

STOLEN BASES

RICKEY HENDERSON	1095
LOU BROCK	938
BILLY HAMILTON	915
TY COBB	892
EDDIE COLLINS	743
ARLIE LATHAM	739
MAX CAREY	738
TIM RAINES	730
HONUS WAGNER	703

JOE MORGAN	689
WILLIE WILSON	660
TOM BROWN	657
BERT CAMPANERIS	649
GEORGE DAVIS	616
VINCE COLEMAN	648
DUMMY HOY	594
MAURY WILLS	586
DAVEY LOPES	557
CESAR CEDENO	550

PINCH HITS

MANNY MOTA	150
SMOKY BURGESS	145
GREG GROSS	143
JOSE MORALES	123
JERRY LYNCH	116
RED LUCAS	114
STEVE BRAUN	113
TERRY CROWLEY	108
GATES BROWN	107
DENNY WALLING	107
MIKE LUM	103
RUSTY STAUB	100
VIC DAVALILLO	95
LARRY BIITTNER	95
JERRY HAIRSTON	94
JIM DWYER	94
DAVE PHILLEY	93
JOEL YOUNGBLOOD	93
JAY JOHNSTONE	92

STRIKEOUTS

REGGIE JACKSON	2597
WILLIE STARGELL	1936
MIKE SCHMIDT	1883
TONY PEREZ	1867
DAVE KINGMAN	1816
BOBBY BONDS	1757
DALE MURPHY	1748
LOU BROCK	1730
MICKEY MANTLE	1710
HARMON KILLEBREW	1699
DWIGHT EVANS	1697
DAVE WINFIELD	1609
LEE MAY	1570
DICK ALLEN	1556
WILLIE MCCOVEY	1550
FRANK ROBINSON	1532
WILLIE MAYS	1526
RICK MONDAY	1513
GREG LUZINSKI	1495

REGULAR SEASON CAREER INDIVIDUAL PITCHING

GAMES

HOYT WILHELM	1070
KENT TEKULVE	1050
LINDY MCDANIEL	987
GOOSE GOSSAGE	966
ROLLIE FINGERS	944
GENE GARBER	931
CY YOUNG	906
SPARKY LYLE	899
JIM KAAT	898
DON MCMAHON	874
JEFF REARDON	869
PHIL NIEKRO	864
LEE SMITH	850
ROY FACE	848
CHARLIE HOUGH	837
TUG MCGRAW	824
NOLAN RYAN	807
DENNIS ECKERSLEY	804
WALTER JOHNSON	801
GAYLORD PERRY	777

INNINGS PITCHED

CY YOUNG	7356
PUD GALVIN	5941
WALTER JOHNSON	5923
PHIL NIEKRO	5403
NOLAN RYAN	5386
GAYLORD PERRY	5351
DON SUTTON	5280
WARREN SPAHN	5244
STEVE CARLTON	5217
GROVER ALEXANDER	5189
KID NICHOLS	5084
TIM KEEFE	5061
BERT BLYLEVEN	4969
MICKEY WELCH	4802
TOM SEAVER	4783
CHRISTY MATHEWSON	4782
TOMMY JOHN	4708
ROBIN ROBERTS	4689
EARLY WYNN	4564
TONY MULLANE	4540

WINS

CY YOUNG	511
WALTER JOHNSON	416
CHRISTY MATHEWSON	373
GROVER ALEXANDER	373
WARREN SPAHN	363

KID NICHOLS 361
PUD GALVIN 361
TIM KEEFE 342
STEVE CARLTON 329
EDDIE PLANK..327
JOHN CLARKSON 326
DON SUTTON..324
NOLAN RYAN 324
PHIL NIEKRO 318
GAYLORD PERRY 314
OLD HOSS RADBOURN...311
TOM SEAVER 311
MICKEY WELCH 308
LEFTY GROVE 300
EARLY WYNN 300

LOSSES

CY YOUNG 315
PUD GALVIN 308
NOLAN RYAN 292
WALTER JOHNSON 279
PHIL NIEKRO 274
GAYLORD PERRY 265
JACK POWELL 256
DON SUTTON..256
EPPA RIXEY 251
BERT BLYLEVEN..250
ROBIN ROBERTS..245
WARREN SPAHN 245
EARLY WYNN 244
STEVE CARLTON 244
JIM KAAT 237
GUS WEYHING 235
FRANK TANANA...234
TOMMY JOHN...231
TED LYONS 230
BOB FRIEND..230

SAVES

LEE SMITH 401
JEFF REARDON 365
ROLLIE FINGERS 341
GOOSE GOSSAGE 309
BRUCE SUTTER 300
DENNIS ECKERSLEY...275
TOM HENKE 260
DAVE RIGHETTI..252
DAN QUISENBERRY 244
SPARKY LYLE...238
JOHN FRANCO...236

EARNED RUN AVERAGE

SHUTOUTS

RUBE WADDELL 50
VIC WILLIS 50

COMPLETE GAMES

CY YOUNG 750
PUD GALVIN 639
TIM KEEFE 557
KID NICHOLS 532
WALTER JOHNSON 531
MICKEY WELCH 525
OLD HOSS RADBOURN 489
JOHN CLARKSON 485
TONY MULLANE 469
TIM McCORMIC 466
GUS WEYHING 448
GROVER ALEXANDER 438
CHRISTY MATHEWSON 435
JACK POWELL 422
EDDIE PLANK...412
WILL WHITE 394
AMOS RUSIE...392
VIC WILLIS..388
WARREN SPAHN 382
JIM WHITNEY..377

STRIKEOUTS

NOLAN RYAN 5714
STEVE CARLTON 4136
BERT BLYLEVEN 3701
TOM SEAVER 3640
DON SUTTON 3574
GAYLORD PERRY 3534
WALTER JOHNSON 3508
PHIL NIEKRO 3342
FERGUSON JENKINS..3192
BOB GIBSON...3117
JIM BUNNING 2855
MICKEY LOLICH..2832
CY YOUNG 2796
FRANK TANANA..2761
WARREN SPAHN 2583
BOB FELLER 2581
JERRY KOOSMAN 2556
TIM KEEFE 2527
CHRISTY MATHEWSON 2502
DON DRYSDALE..2486

BASES ON BALLS

NOLAN RYAN 2795
STEVE CARLTON 1833
PHIL NIEKRO 1809
EARLY WYNN 1775
BOB FELLER 1764

BOBO NEWSOM	1732
AMOS RUSIE	1704
CHARLIE HOUGH	1613
GUS WEYHING	1566
RED RUFFING	1541
BUMP HADLEY	1442
WARREN SPAHN	1434
EARL WHITEHILL	1431
TONY MULLANE	1409
SAD SAM JONES	1396
TOM SEAVER	1390
GAYLORD PERRY	1379
MIKE TORREZ	1371
WALTER JOHNSON	1355
DON SUTTON	1343

HALL OF FAME MANAGERS

	YEARS MANAGED	YEAR SELECTED
WALT ALSTON	1954-76	1983
CLARK GRIFFITH	1901-20	1946
BUCKY HARRIS	1924-56	1975
MILLER HUGGINS	1913-29	1964
AL LOPEZ	1951-69	1977
CONNIE MACK	1894-1950	1937
JOE MCCARTHY	1926-50	1957
JOHN MCGRAW	1899-1932	1937
BILL MCKECHNIE	1915-46	1962
WILBERT ROBINSON	1902-31	1945
CASEY STENGEL	1934-65	1966

NATIONAL BASEBALL HALL OF FAME & MUSEUM

ADDRESS: P.O. BOX 590, COOPERSTOWN, N.Y. 13326
PHONE: (607) 547-9988